The
Art
of
Inventing
Hope

The
Art
of
Inventing
Hope

Intimate Conversations with

ELIE WIESEL

HOWARD REICH

CHICAGO
REVIEW
PRESS

Published by Chicago Review Press Incorporated
814 North Franklin Street
Chicago, Illinois 60610
ISBN 978-1-64160-134-4

Library of Congress Cataloging-in-Publication Data
Names: Reich, Howard, author.
Title: The art of inventing hope : intimate conversations with Elie Wiesel /
  Howard Reich.
Description: Chicago, Illinois : Chicago Review Press Incorporated, [2019] |
  Includes index.
Identifiers: LCCN 2018035541| ISBN 9781641601344 (cloth) |
  ISBN 9781641601375 (epub) | ISBN 9781641601368 (kindle)
Subjects: LCSH: Holocaust survivors. | Wiesel, Elie, 1928–2016. | Children of
  Holocaust survivors. | Reich, Howard. | Holocaust, Jewish (1939–1945)
Classification: LCC D804.3 .R437 2019 | DDC 940.53/18092—dc23
  LC record available at https://lccn.loc.gov/2018035541

Typesetting: Nord Compo

Printed in the United States of America
5 4 3 2 1

For Pam Becker, my wife, who makes all things possible.
And for Amanda Abramovitz, my niece,
the next writer in our family and the inheritor of its story.

Contents

Preface

We are sitting alone together on the stage of Orchestra Hall in Chicago—upward of twenty-five hundred people in the audience—but neither one of us was supposed to be here. Or anywhere.

Elie Wiesel was marked for death in Auschwitz-Birkenau and later, at the end of the war, in Buchenwald. My father, Robert Reich, very nearly died of beatings, typhus, and starvation in various concentration camps, his ordeals also culminating in Buchenwald.

But these two men—who perhaps brushed past each other in a place that held some of the last Eastern European Jews still alive early in 1945—somehow survived, making possible many other lives, including my own.

And so Wiesel and I find ourselves onstage on a sunny and crisp November morning in 2012 as he receives the Chicago Tribune Literary Award, an honor given by the newspaper where I have worked my entire career. With the audience hushed and not a single cell phone daring to go off, Wiesel answers my questions, telling me and an obviously intrigued audience his story, which ultimately is my story and the story of all children of survivors.

For most of my life, I never knew the tale. My father, who died in 1991 at age sixty-nine, said very little about what happened to him during the war, and my mother, Sonia Reich—also a survivor—even less. This was not a subject much discussed in the 1950s, when I was growing up. Yes, survivors talked to each other constantly about their tragedies—in Yiddish, Hebrew, Polish, Hungarian, German, Russian, broken English, and whatnot. Practically every conversation, they have told me since, sooner or later (and usually sooner) circled back to life and death in the camps, to grieving those who were lost, to the world's staggering indifference. But rare was the parent who sat a child down and conveyed what had occurred.

How could they? How could they possibly have put into words the horrors, fears, traumas, and chaos that words had no chance of containing?

And yet somehow Wiesel managed to capture a sense of the darkness and dread of what he simply and starkly calls the Experience, in his book *Night* and in many less-familiar works as well, most notably *The Gates of the Forest, The Fifth Son,* and *The Forgotten,* and in his two volumes of memoirs, *All Rivers Run to the Sea* and *And the Sea Is Never Full,* plus dozens of articles and speeches.

Until three months before our conversation in Orchestra Hall, however, I hadn't read a word of these works, or anything else by Wiesel. Holocaust literature was not required reading when I went to school, and anyway, I had gone out of my way most of my life to avoid the subject. It was too frightening, too onerous, too unspeakable, too incomprehensible, too tautly wrapped up in pain and guilt and morbidity for me to touch. I feared it. I froze whenever I heard the *H* word.

But something happened on the night of February 15, 2001, to abruptly change all of that and, in a way, to lead to my very public conversation with Wiesel. My mother's Holocaust past—about which she had told my sister and me perhaps three sentences as we were growing up—reemerged on that freezing February evening. Believing killers were pursuing her again, my then sixty-nine-year-old mother packed two shopping bags full of clothes and fled the little house in which she and my father had raised us in the Chicago suburb of Skokie, a nexus of Holocaust survivors. After roaming the streets for God knows how long, my mother was picked up by the local police, to whom she insisted someone was trying to "put a bullet" in her head, she said.

In effect, she had begun reliving her Holocaust. It took a year for me to find a doctor who diagnosed what should have been obvious to all the psychiatrists who brushed her off: she was suffering from post-traumatic stress disorder, and no one recognized it. Not even me. Her past was coming back to haunt her, in the form of delusion.

Or maybe I shouldn't call it delusion, since once it really did happen.

Suddenly the terrible subject that I had worked so assiduously to avoid all my life was staring me in the face, and there was no avoiding it anymore. I had to get help for my mother, and I needed to find out not only why she was reenacting her childhood in flight but also what had happened to her. It turned out that there was nothing that could be done to alleviate my mother's terrors, but I certainly could vow to find their source.

My search took me to Warsaw, where I discovered the family my mother never told me about, and to the tiny village of Dubno, now in Western Ukraine but then in easternmost Poland. I learned that of the twelve thousand Jews who had lived in my mother's town before the war, fewer than one hundred were believed to have escaped machine-gun killings conducted by the Nazi Einsatzgruppe C—the same band of executioners that would kill many more en route to the notorious massacre at Babi Yar.

Somehow my mother had escaped this death, spending her adolescence running and hiding from a society determined to kill her for being a Jew. Afterward, in the United States, she tried to put her past behind her as much as possible—until it erupted anew on that February night in 2001.

I'm sure it was because of my writings on my mother's story and on those of other survivors that the *Tribune* asked me to conduct the public interview with Wiesel, our lives now linked not just by the Buchenwald past he shared with my father but also by my quest to learn more—which, of course, had been his mission all along. In a way, our meeting was well timed, if you can say that about anything related to the Holocaust. For though I eventually learned nearly everything possible about my mother's past (short of her telling me in her own words, which she clearly could not), I now had more questions than when I started out.

I wondered how my parents and the others endured. Where did they find the strength to start over? How did they cope with the overwhelming destruction of their families, friends, and shtetls? Why did almost no one help them? How was it possible to believe in God after the Holocaust? Or during? Why did the survivors have children? Why didn't the world want to hear the survivors' stories after the war?

And what were we, the children of the survivors, to make of all this? What did we lose by not having grandparents? What do we do about the stories we never heard? How do we deal with the guilt of knowing—or imagining—our parents' suffering? How do we manage being involuntary inheritors of tragedy, grief, and heroism? How has this legacy affected us? How should we speak of the Holocaust today? What is our responsibility? What do we tell our children? What do we do with this legacy if we have no children?

How do we listen to the music of Wagner, which provided the de facto soundtrack for the Holocaust? Or should we?

An avalanche of questions emerged as I studied and chronicled my mother's unspoken past. The more I learned, the more I needed to know.

And who better to ask than Wiesel? I began devouring his books and articles in preparation for meeting him for the first time in New York, in October 2012, and for our public conversation in Chicago a month later.

To say that we spoke the same language would be an understatement. He answered questions that had been playing in my mind—some of which I'd never said aloud—with poetic clarity. And after our Orchestra Hall appearance, the conversation continued. It had to. By phone and in person, in Chicago and New York and Florida, I needed to ask him more. He agreed, often ending our conversations with the best possible phrase I could have asked to hear: "To be continued."

I don't pretend that my research and writings have helped my mother or late father a bit, except insofar as their stories—and those of all the survivors—demand to be told and retold. But I hope that my conversations with Wiesel, which have helped me struggle with the event that shaped my life more than any other, can benefit readers.

Not that the words between these covers diminish the pain and burden of what happened. I mean only that my precious time with Wiesel over those four years, until his death in 2016 at age eighty-seven, has helped me try to learn to speak about unspeakable events, a difficult task even at this late date.

Wiesel was a guide to me in grappling with questions that perhaps have no answers but require our pursuit nonetheless. Especially if you are a child or grandchild of survivors. If you're not, surely Wiesel's wisdom also has value, for he addressed ideas that carry implications for all of humanity; his experiences during the Holocaust and his writings and advocacy thereafter offer lessons to us all.

But before I can unfurl my first questions, I must tell you what it was like growing up in a family of Holocaust survivors for whom, I came to realize relatively late in life, the Holocaust never really ended.

1

The Holocaust Returns

It's the middle of the night, and I should be asleep, but I've gotten out of bed for a drink of water. I'm ten years old and living in our squat but, to us, luxurious ranch house in Skokie, Illinois. As I take a few steps out of my bedroom, which is just a few steps from every other room, I see exactly what I expect: my mother sitting on the floor in the darkened living room, her petite silhouette outlined by soft yellow light trickling in from the streetlamp outside. As always, she has lifted the window shade a couple inches above the sill, so she can peer out and watch the occasional car drive silently by.

She's always there when I get out of bed at night, when I feel ill and call out for help, whenever she's needed, really. She doesn't seem to sleep—certainly not in bed, as far as I can tell. Instead she keeps a nightly vigil in our living room and has done so for as long as I can remember. In fact, I figure all moms must spend each night in front of the living room window, guarding everyone else.

But this is not the only nocturnal ritual in our house. Often my father gets out of bed and proceeds directly to the breakfront in our dining room, opens the bottom cabinet door, lifts up a bottle of whiskey, twists out the cork, and draws a few swallows. Then he methodically recorks the fifth, puts it away, closes the cabinet door, and heads back to bed, saying not a word to my mother as he passes her. Or at least none that I can hear. Sometimes he does this two or three times a night.

He'll have to get out of bed for good soon anyway, because long before sunrise, he'll need to drive to the bakery where he works in Chicago, and the alcohol helps him sleep. Or helps him try.

On weekends, though, he gets to sleep later in the morning, and often when he wakes up, he tells us about his dreams.

"I was killing Nazis good," he says, with an air of triumph. "I was shooting them down."

I know that my dad and mom have survived what they briefly told me was the Holocaust, that most of their relatives were executed for being Jews, that my parents had to start over here, in America, and that they feel lucky for that, as if they'd hit the jackpot. But that's about all I know. And, frankly, it's all I want to know. If machine-gunning Nazis in his dreams makes my dad happy, that's fine with me. Sounds like an Audie Murphy movie.

As I look back on it, though, those early years in Skokie—and a few in Chicago before that—were haunted by the Holocaust in ways I did not recognize or understand at the time. We were never supposed to take showers, for instance, though my parents didn't tell me why. Our Skokie house had a perfectly fine—if compact—working bathroom, but showers were categorically banned. My friends took showers, people on TV and in movies took showers, apparently everyone in America took showers, except us. Only baths. It wasn't until I was much older that I came to learn what showers signified for my mother and father.

When my father would talk to his survivor relatives on the telephone, the conversations often would devolve into screaming matches, someone inevitably smashing down the handset on the other party. Yet when we would go out on weekends, we would socialize exclusively with these same relatives who a few days earlier had been berating each other on the other end of the soon-to-be-slammed-down phone. If these relatives couldn't stand each other that much, I often wondered in my naïveté, why were they getting together all the time? These survivors, who had experienced the worst that humanity had to offer, clearly trusted no one, not even each other. And yet they apparently found some kind of solace in each other's company, even amid their raging battles.

When I misbehaved, my parents and aunts and uncles sent Holocaust references my way without shedding much light on the subject. "You wouldn't last ten minutes in the Holocaust," an aunt would say. "You should kiss the ground every day that you have a mother and a father—do you know what I would give to have my parents?" my dad would snarl. "He doesn't know how good he has it," my mother would echo. "When I was your age, I was sleeping in the snow. But he has a big mouth to his parents."

I didn't realize it then, but these people understandably were bursting with anger about what had happened to them and their families, their fury directed at anyone and everyone who happened to wander into their line of fire. Their passions poured forth at whomever was closest, and that, of course, was each other, and me. They had lost faith in virtually everyone, even blood relatives who had suffered through the same trials as them. I guess all of them had learned—under dire circumstances—what people are capable of, and they could not forget it.

Still, coming to Skokie in 1964 was the greatest event in my family's life to that point, and not necessarily because so many survivors had moved there. No one really knew that fact at that time, anyway. Not until the late 1970s would the survivors in Skokie rise up as a group to be heard when famously confronted by neo-Nazis who threatened to march there, causing a worldwide media sensation.

No, Skokie was magical to us because of how far we had come to reach this place of impeccably trimmed lawns and bright, spotless streets.

In 1947, two years after the war, my mother arrived in Chicago as a sixteen-year-old educated only to age eight and now left practically to fend for herself without knowing a syllable of English. My father came to Chicago in 1949 at age twenty-seven, having spent the first year after the war in Germany recuperating from typhus and the effects of years of deprivations and abuse. The two met on a blind date in Chicago and in 1953 got married, a pair of Holocaust survivors whose shared histories surely bonded them as nothing else could.

In the mid-1950s, they opened a bakery with my father's brother in Chicago's Germantown, Holocaust survivors choosing to run a business in the heart of the culture that had destroyed most of their families and decimated their people. That may seem odd, but, looking back on it, I suppose it made a strange kind of sense, from their point of view. My father and his brother, after all, had grown up in a family of bakers in Poland, and my father had trained as a baker in Germany after the war. Both spoke Deutsch fluently and knew how to bake German breads, pastries, and other delicacies just like the natives. How else were they to make a living in a strange country? And where else in Chicago could they better ply their trade than in Germantown?

What seemed a bit weird to me was that everyone—my parents, aunts, and uncles—told me that I was not supposed to reveal to anyone that we were Jewish. They swore me to secrecy. Neither teachers nor classmates nor, above all, customers were to be told the truth. Clearly my parents feared that if anyone in Germantown knew that we were Jews—let alone that my parents had survived the Final Solution conceived in Germany and exported widely—who knew what would happen? Even in the 1950s, even in America, my parents feared revealing their true identities.

All of which was fine with me. I learned to speak German from my German babysitter, and I never got near a synagogue or a yarmulke or a prayer book or anything else remotely Jewish. Every day after school, my babysitter took me to church, where I learned to pray as a Catholic, making the gesture of the cross with my right arm traveling from shoulder to shoulder and head to torso and lighting the candles at the altar.

Unfortunately our bakery went bust with the recession of the late 1950s, and my dad quickly got a job working at someone else's bakery. That meant we moved to East Rogers Park, a gritty neighborhood on the north side of Chicago, and then, like thousands of other survivor families, on to the Promised Land, also known as Skokie.

The small suburb just north of Chicago was trying to grow into a bedroom community and explicitly sought out Jews who long had been unwelcome in suburbs ringing Chicago and beyond. One survivor told another and another, and by the '70s, Skokie would be home to an estimated seven to eight thousand of them—more than 10 percent of the population of a town already more than half Jewish—all living in a village barely ten miles square.

Once we arrived, my parents finally announced themselves as Jews. I watched my dad proudly nail a mezuzah to the doorway. We joined a nearby temple and lit the menorah every Hanukkah. I went to Hebrew school. I studied for my bar mitzvah. We were not in danger.

Each night, when my father went to sleep, he would say to me, "Do you know how I feel when I put my head on this pillow? Like a millionaire!" Each night, he must have thought of how he had tried to sleep in Buchenwald, never knowing if he would live through the next day.

Despite the oasis my parents and other survivors found in Skokie—which they transformed into a modern-day shtetl crowded with synagogues, Hebrew schools, and delis—they mostly kept their dark histories to themselves. Sure, during summer you'd sometimes see men and women in short sleeves with blue numbers etched on the inside of their forearms, but somehow you knew not to ask about it.

My dad and his surviving brothers and sister had no such numbers, so it was a long time before I learned that this was a particular mark of Auschwitz. When children asked their parents about the tattoos, many survivors told me decades later, the survivors often said they'd simply written down their phone numbers so they wouldn't forget.

So even though Skokie eventually would become one of the world's most famous—or infamous—sanctuaries for survivors, they kept such a low profile that hardly anyone outside their circle knew they were there.

"Nobody ever rolled up their sleeve and showed me a tattooed number," Mort Paradise, a World War II veteran who moved to Skokie in 1949, once told me. "They probably had no motivation to broadcast the fact that they were survivors."

None indeed.

That is, until neo-Nazi Frank Collin began threatening to march with his brown-shirted, swastika-wearing colleagues on the streets of Skokie. Of all places. WE ARE COMING read the flyers they started distributing widely in September 1976, the picture showing "a caricature of a swastika reaching out to throttle a stereotyped Eastern European ghetto Jew," wrote Philippa Strum in her book *When the Nazis Came to Skokie*. Collin and friends vowed to provide "the final solution to the Jewish question," and the survivors did not take this promise lightly. The rapidly rising tensions made Collin a media phenomenon; newspapers and TV stations from around the globe covered the spectacle of it all.

"We were getting calls, here at my house, in the middle of the night, from people living in countries far and wide, who asked what they could do," Skokie's then village attorney Harvey Schwartz once told me. "Could they send us money? Could they send us bullets? Anything to stop this."

My dad was burning up, his face turning white whenever Collin and friends appeared on TV or in the papers, which was practically nonstop in 1977 and '78. I was confounded that my family would take this clown seriously, but I later came to understand why. Hitler, too, had been considered a buffoon until he was duly elected chancellor of Germany in 1933 and began setting the stage for the annihilation of a people.

Though Skokie officials at first suggested that everyone simply pull down their window shades and ignore the planned march, the survivors refused. Thunderously. Early on they gathered at Village Hall, more than one hundred strong, determined to be heard, while Collin took his First Amendment case for his right to march to the courts.

"Many of them stood in shock, catatonic, unable to move," village attorney Schwartz told me, weeping at the memory. "What I realized at that moment was that what we were facing had nothing to do with the First Amendment. When someone wants to come marching into your town, with the announced intention to kill you, there was hardly anything left to discuss."

Neither my dad nor many of the survivors were going to let the Nazis return, even if it meant meeting Collin in the streets.

"I'll get a bat and break his head if he marches," my dad often said.

I believed him.

"We told the police, 'In case they will come in, they're going to be dead,'" survivor Ben Kryska once said to me. "We all had guns."

Each time Collin threatened to march, survivors waited for him on the upper stories of buildings facing Oakton Street, the main boulevard in downtown Skokie, trigger fingers ready, aiming dead ahead.

Luckily no shooting ever happened. Collin's case, tirelessly championed by the American Civil Liberties Union, made it all the way to the United States Supreme Court.

Elie Wiesel would not be silent about this turn of events.

"In its preoccupation with the rights of the Nazis," Wiesel wrote in *Newsday* in 1978, "the ACLU neglected those of their intended victims. Are they not worthy of the same concern? Are they not entitled to equal protection—or at least to compassion? After all, they are threatened, not the Nazis. They are in danger, not the Nazis. They are wounded, not the Nazis. They have nightmares, not the Nazis. Is there no law to defend them as well, and, if not, why hasn't the ACLU sought to do something in the matter?"

With the ACLU's help, the Nazis indeed prevailed under the law; the Supreme Court affirmed their First Amendment right to march. But Collin never exercised it, taking his message of group hatred to Humboldt Park and downtown Chicago instead. Why? He never said, but my guess is that he knew the survivors would be waiting for him, and that there was a very good chance the Skokie police would look the other way.

Years later, after all the neo-Nazi noise, Collin was sentenced to prison for child molestation and gave himself a new name and identity. But he surely had succeeded in retraumatizing thousands of survivors, like my parents, who had come to Skokie believing they had escaped the horrors of the past once and for all.

Collin reminded them that they never really would.

But the survivors were galvanized, many of them resolving never to let such a travesty occur again. They organized a speakers' bureau that opened in a storefront museum three blocks from our Skokie house in 1984. They lobbied to make Illinois the first state in the country to require Holocaust education in public elementary and high schools in 1990. And their decidedly unglamorous headquarters, located in a former dental-supplies building next door to a tavern, morphed into the $65 million Illinois Holocaust Museum and Education Center elsewhere in the suburb.

"Has the world learned the lesson?" Wiesel said at the opening ceremony, on April 19, 2009, the sixty-sixth anniversary of the Warsaw ghetto uprising and, coincidentally, my birthday.

"Sadly, the answer is no."

I hadn't started to learn such lessons, however, until that frozen night my mother ran out of her house. At first, I thought she was suffering from Alzheimer's or some other form of dementia. The psychiatrists who evaluated her in Skokie were equally clueless. Though my mother's hospital admittance records plainly identified her as a Holocaust survivor who "states that she is seeing animals and dogs chasing her," she was diagnosed with "delusional disorder" and dispatched to an assisted-living center. No one connected her "delusions" with her autobiography. Incredible.

So my journey to find out what happened began. An aunt of my mother's who lived in New Jersey, Irene Tannen, provided fragments of information on my mother's past and suggested I visit my mother's cousin, Leon Slominski, in Warsaw, to learn more.

My mother had family in Warsaw? That was news to me. Slominski helped fill in the story, our conversations in Poland inevitably leading me to the town where he and my mother and their aunt were born and very nearly executed. War crimes reports and eye witnesses I found in Dubno, as well as additional research at the United States Holocaust Memorial Museum in Washington, told me what no one ever had.

On September 17, 1939, shortly after Hitler and Stalin had decided to divide Poland between them by signing a nonaggression pact, Soviet tanks rolled into "my little Dubno," as my mother called her birthplace. The Soviets nationalized property and took over homes, including the one my mother, her aunt, and the extended family lived in. The soldiers pushed them all into a single room in back, a few steps from the outhouse in the yard.

This is what my mother learned can happen to you when you're eight years old.

Two years later, when Hitler broke the deal with Stalin and invaded Eastern Poland, bombs began dropping on Dubno at 4:00 AM on June 22, 1941. My mother was ten, and the family home must have trembled. The Nazis arrived via tank three days later, which is when the executions in and around Dubno began, select Jews machine-gunned at a sacred place: the Jewish cemetery.

The killing continued, according to war crimes reports the Soviets wrote after liberating Dubno in 1944.

"This day we arrived at the excavation site, 4 km west of Dubno in the direction of the village of Kleschikha, in the vicinity of the Shibennaya Hill, where in a gorge we discovered corpses of shot and killed peaceful people of Jewish nationality from the Dubno, Verba and Ostrozhets districts," noted a report dated December 1944. "The total area of all three pits is 900 sq. m, 4 m deep," it continued, "where there are 6,000 shot and killed people. During the excavation, it has been found that there are six to seven layers of corpses of shot people, lying with their faces down. Each layer has up to 21 rows of shot and killed people and is covered with chlorinated lime.

"The fact that the corpses are naked and lie with their faces down indicates that the shots were aimed at the back of the head and the rear area of the thorax; this is corroborated by the fact that the bullet entry hole was found in the back of the head and between the blades. The killing execution of Jewish population took place on 07.27.1941. The second time—07.30.1941. The third execution—08.22.1941. The fourth execution—07.27.1942. The fifth execution—10.6.1942, when 3,000 people were killed. The last execution was conducted 10.24.1942; over 1,000 people were killed that day."

By that last October date, the ghetto the Nazis had established on April 2, 1942—the first day of Passover—was bloodied and empty (though executions in the region continued until 1944). My mother's aunt Irene and her cousin Leon remembered that my mother was still in the ghetto when they fled, which means that sometime between the summer and fall of 1942, my mother escaped as well. She once had told me that her mother instructed her to run, hoping the young child would survive. "I was running, running, I didn't know where I was running," my mother said, one of the few things she ever revealed about her secret childhood.

My mother spent the next three years in flight. She was "thrust into a bizarrely hostile world and became a hunted animal, 'a jungle child,' who barely survived by the use of running, hiding and begging," wrote Dr. David Rosenberg, the Chicago-area psychiatrist who ultimately diagnosed her PTSD a year after the doctors in Skokie failed to.

Somehow, toward the end of the war, my mother found her aunt, and they spent the last year hiding together under false papers in southern Poland. After the war, they learned that just a few in an extended family of dozens had survived: Irene's sister Fira and my mother's cousins Leon and his sister Fanka were among those who lived. The rest—parents, aunts, uncles, dozens more—slaughtered.

It had taken me more than a year to piece together this story, but I still knew almost nothing about what happened to my father. When I dug into our family's safe-deposit box at the bank, I saw—for the first time—a brief affidavit he had submitted in applying for restitution from the German government after the war. The document offered, in succinct but harrowing detail, an outline of my father's terrible journey from a beautiful childhood in Sosnowiec, Poland, to a then-unimagined fate.

"In September, 1939, when the German soldiers came to Sosnowiec, they immediately took over my father's bakery, and I was forced to work there," my father wrote. "Jews were allowed to walk only on certain streets and to take certain street cars. We were forbidden to leave the city. In September of 1939, I was forced to wear a Judenstern, a white armband with a blue star on it. I wore the Judenstern from September of 1939 until I arrived in the Markstadt Work Camp in February of 1942. . . . S.S. men were stationed throughout Sosnowiec, and we knew we would be shot if orders were disobeyed."

In the Markstadt work camp, where my father labored for a year starting in February 1942, he subsisted in barracks with more than two dozen other men.

"I was given food once a day, either bread or soup," he wrote. "I had to stand in line many hours for this. Factories were being built outside the work camp, and I was forced to work in the building of them."

My father's agonies began at 5:00 AM, he wrote, the prisoners marching an hour to work, then laboring from 6:00 AM to 6:00 PM, six days a week. He was forced to carry heavy asbestos plates that were used for roofing.

In February 1943, under SS guard, he and the others were marched to the Funfteichen concentration camp, which held thousands of men. Here my father survived in a barracks with approximately two hundred others, all garbed in the familiar striped uniform of concentration camp prisoners, fed "ersatz coffee and bread in the morning and very weak soup at night," he wrote. He worked at the same pace in the same manner as before, lifting asbestos plates up to the roof, as well as building railroad beds and loading sand into dump cars.

Beatings "and other types of cruelty" were delivered often and arbitrarily by SS guards, my father wrote, the conditions so severe that he estimated one hundred men died each week. Sometime in 1943 or '44 he "was hit over the head . . . resulting in a scar, fell down, was unconscious, came to in the barracks," according to his affidavit.

In January 1945, as the war was grinding to its finish, my father and the others still barely living were sent on a death march to Buchenwald. About six thousand men began this journey, which lasted two weeks, and about two hundred lived to the end of it, my father estimated in his testimony. The men were given no food or water along the way. They marched in snow.

"We were given no blankets and had to sleep out-of-doors or packed like cattle in barns. S.S. troops guarded us constantly," my father wrote. "If a man fell he was shot to death where he had fallen. . . . About four days before the end of the march, the remaining men and I were packed in open cattle cars and taken to the Buchenwald Concentration Camp."

My father was sick when he arrived at Buchenwald, he wrote, "but I did not report this, as I was afraid I might be sent to a crematorium." He and the others were ordered to stand in line for hours to be counted, he reported. The rest of the time, they worked at a variety of tasks. "Sometimes I was forced to throw dead bodies on to wagons."

On April 11, 1945, my father, Elie Wiesel, and the others who inexplicably survived all of this were liberated from Buchenwald by the United States Army. Even after spending nearly a year recovering, my father was left with lifelong pain.

"The entire right side, the shoulder, the elbow, the entire side always hurts," he wrote. "I carried so many slabs."

How do you restart a life after that? How do you get past such inconceivable loss and suffering, move to another country, learn a language, get a job, raise a family, continue? How is that possible? And how do you tell your children?

My parents never did, and it had taken me a long time—too long—to inquire. In fact, I now realize, I didn't really explore the subject until my father was gone and my mother was only partially connected to reality. In a way, I guess you could say I couldn't bear to look at this when they were still in their prime, as if the information would be too difficult to face in that situation. Or maybe that's just a nice way of putting it, a kind of rationalization of my avoidance of the subject.

Knowing what I had learned, my visits to my mother in the nursing home where she has been living since 2001 became more saddening but also more poignant. For though I never really found out what happened to her during those missing years when she was running for her life, I certainly learned a great deal about who she was: a kind of hero who wanted no plaudits or even recognition for what she had endured. She and my father wanted only to live and to create life.

Yet it seemed unbearably unjust that now my mother was reliving the terrors of her past, in ways that were unnerving to observe. For the first several years in the nursing home, my mother slept every night fully dressed, seated in the chair next to her bed, which she refused to use. She kept a bag next to her packed with toothbrush, toothpaste, and what she quaintly called "unmentionables," in case she suddenly had to flee. And, once again, she spent her nights looking out the window.

Only when her health began to fail did she allow the nurses to put her to bed after dark. Even so, she insisted that there was a Star of David on her clothes and mine, that people were trying to kill us both, but that she believed we ultimately would survive. Repeatedly, and to this day, she says to me, "I am not a whore—I was a married woman," suggesting scenarios from her past that I dare not think of.

Often she tells me how deeply she believes in God. In spite of everything. Or maybe because of it.

Yet her life remains precarious, frightful, fraught.

Once, when she apparently was lost in her belief that the past had returned, she said these indelible words to me: "Where the night catches me, there I sleep. Where the day catches me, there I live."

Of course I had to write all of this down, which I did in several *Tribune* articles, a book, and a documentary film. Which led me, inexorably but surprisingly, to Wiesel.

One afternoon, as I arrived on the scene of an unrelated story in Chicago, my cell phone rang. "I wanted to bounce an idea off of you," said Scott Powers, one of my editors at the newspaper.

Sure.

"The *Tribune* is giving the Literary Award this year to Elie Wiesel," he said, and instantly I understood the implications of that sentence—or at least some of them.

I obviously was going to be asked if I'd like to interview the Nobel Peace Prize laureate for a *Tribune* story and, I guessed, for the traditional public conversation on the stage of Orchestra Hall.

"Would you be interested?" said the editor.

Yes. Yes, indeed.

Two weeks later, I would be dialing Wiesel's number in New York to do a brief phone interview for a short article I would write announcing the award. I promised myself that when I spoke to him, I would not bring up my parents' story. This was not about them or me—it was about him.

But it didn't take more than a few minutes for him to tease out the truth. "What do you do at the *Tribune*?" he asked, after I had finished my basic interview questions.

"I write about music," I said, noting that I had been a *Tribune* arts critic for decades.

"Then why are you doing this story?"

That was fast. I quickly told him of my parents' history, my family's journey through the Holocaust, my efforts to find their story, and my writings on the subject.

"Send me the book," he said. "We'll talk when you come to New York."

We would.

2

A Troubled Inheritance

The slender, silver-haired gentleman appeared in the small lobby of his Manhattan office suite to greet me. He wore a light gray suit, crisply pressed shirt, and tie on that morning of October 17, 2012, our first meeting. We smiled and shook hands, and as he escorted me back to his office, I saw that the narrow corridor we were walking through—as well as the other rooms I peeked into—was lined with bookcases, each packed to overflowing.

His office looked like a library, even the coffee table piled three or four deep with tomes. There certainly wasn't any room for a cup of coffee. He invited me to sit on the sofa while he took a spot kitty-corner from me on an adjacent chair, our knees bumping up against each other.

Immediately Elie Wiesel asked about my mother. He wanted to know more about her story, more about how she was reliving her past—and, in a way, his. I recapped it for him, and he listened attentively, not saying a word.

Finally he spoke. "I know people like that," he said. "Which is actually normal."

Normal? By that I presumed he meant that the way my mother was behaving now—after all she had experienced and suffered—wasn't really so strange after all. Maybe he was right. Why wouldn't someone be terrified after enduring such events? Why wouldn't someone be undone by such memories?

"How can you uproot it, an event that affected history in its very depth, somebody who went through it?" Wiesel asked.

To feel persecuted and endangered really was a kind of normal for my mother, he seemed to be saying, a perspective I had not considered until that moment. In effect, I'd been comparing my mother to *my* normal and to society's normal, but not to hers. The fears that had gripped her as a child never really left, I was learning, and how oblivious of me to have presumed they had. How naive to have gone about my childhood and adulthood as if everything were pretty much OK.

Sure, as I got older I'd realized that moms looking out the window all night and dads dreaming of mowing down Nazis were not the stuff of Norman Rockwell paintings. But it all seemed quirky and a little odd rather than profoundly disturbing, as I had belatedly come to realize it was.

Thus my conversation with Wiesel began in earnest, the two of us speaking of a subject that had dominated both our lives, though I had been quite late to understand that. We spoke easily, like friends who have a shared history and common memories, even though we had shaken hands for the first time just moments ago.

Not five minutes went by, in fact, before he took me inside his family and his story. Here's what happened: I'd asked him why, when he was liberated from Buchenwald, he had immediately requested pen and paper, as I'd learned from his memoirs? Why the urgent need to write?

"I always wrote," he said, referencing his interrupted youth in Sighet, Transylvania, in what is now Romania.

"I'll tell you something—I had two older sisters and a smaller one, Tzipora. The oldest ones survived, but I didn't know that they survived. One of them went back to Sighet after the war, hoping to meet me. At that time, there were no connections; there were no communications, telephones. We didn't have anything.

"She thought maybe I survived. And she found certain things in Sighet. And she found—actually I'll show it to you. My older sister [recently] died, and her son sent me what I'm going to show you now. Of all the writings, this is one that gives me palpitations."

With that, Wiesel rose up from his chair and walked across the room to his desk, pulled from inside a top drawer a tiny yellow tablet, maybe four inches by two inches, walked back over to me, sat down again, and revealed to me what he held tenderly with the fingertips of both hands.

"You are the only outsider, surely journalist, I show this to," he said.

"I wrote in Hebrew," he added, referring to the handwritten lettering I saw. "Nineteen forty-one: These are all reflections on mysticism in our prayers. At thirteen."

On these pages, in the year of his bar mitzvah, a young Elie Wiesel had documented his thoughts onto this little tablet of paper, and somehow it came through the Holocaust intact, while most of Wiesel's family, and mine, did not.

"Can you imagine this survived?" he said to me, still marveling at what he held.

Now, in this moment, two people born on opposite moments of the same event—before and after—began speaking to each other with an intimacy I had not anticipated. If Wiesel was willing to show me this precious document, to share with me this fragile shard of his past, then surely he wouldn't mind if I asked him more: about his life, his writings, his frustrations at believing he had not been able to do justice to a subject for which everyone turned to him for understanding, now including me: the Holocaust.

And so the avalanche of questions began. I asked him why the world did not help. Why people didn't want to hear the survivors' stories. Why most survivors didn't talk about the subject publicly for so long. Why genocide still rages around the globe. How the survivors stayed sane. How he stayed sane. Whether the story will endure after the survivors are gone.

None of these inquiries, of course, could have been answered fully in a single meeting or two or three. But a month later we continued our dialogue on the stage of Orchestra Hall in Chicago, and the conversation continued for four years afterward. I had much to learn.

I quickly discovered that my plan to ask Wiesel the questions I had never asked my parents—questions I should have asked—was considerably less original than I thought. Others of my generation, the second generation, had come to him as well, bringing him queries they did not or could not or would not ask their parents, he told me. And they reached him much earlier than I did, signing up for his classes at the City College of New York as early as the 1970s, when I was still running away from a subject they were running toward.

"I became a kind of surrogate," Wiesel said to me. "What their fathers didn't tell them, they wanted me to tell them.

"How did I find out?" that his students were children of survivors, he asked rhetorically. "The parents came to see me," and they told him. "And I had one student, the best student in the class. At that time, it was very modern to be a hippie. He was a hippie. Marvelous student, one of the best, but a hippie.

"And he said to me, 'Look, professor, you must understand. I'm the only son. But my father had a wife and children before me. My mother had a husband and children before the war. They were all killed. But my father and my mother married after the war, and they gave birth to one son: me.'

"Phew," said Wiesel, still struck by the onus on this young man.

Then Wiesel continued his story, recalling what his prized student had said about coping with his parents' history.

"He said, 'Each morning when I see them, can you imagine what I have in my head?'" Wiesel recounted.

As he said these words, I thought, *Yes, I can.* I can imagine my mother, a girl barely eleven years old being sent out of the ghetto by her mother and told to run, just run. I can imagine, or try to, the terrors she experienced, the chaos and confusion and nihilism of her young life, the humiliations, the eternity that three years in flight must have seemed like to a girl just entering her adolescence. Time moves slowly at that age, and surely even more slowly amid such cruelties.

I can imagine, too, my father in Buchenwald, emaciated, sick with typhus, fevered. As Wiesel spoke, in fact, I began to remember a story my father had told me of his last days there. The anecdote was vague and incomplete in my mind, but I recalled my father saying that toward the end of the war the Nazis had come to take some Jews out of the camp to go God knows where. And my father said he began acting as if he were having a fit of delirium or epilepsy. He was flailing, hysterical, he said. Crazy. On that day, the Nazis surprisingly left him alone. As my father told me this story, he smiled a little, proud that he had outwitted his captors and managed to live for one more day.

No, it is not hard for us, the children of survivors, to imagine.

Wiesel continued telling me of his encounters with the children of survivors.

One student came to speak with him privately and started "crying and crying and crying," unable to halt the deluge, Wiesel said.

Another time, a parent came to share with Wiesel one of the most difficult stories a parent can tell. Her son, she said, had been trying to write down his parents' Holocaust history and finally "went into the ocean with the typewriter around his neck and drowned," said Wiesel. The parent told him this, he presumed, "so I could imagine the despair of the children."

If you are a child of a survivor, the story is always there with you, whether you recognize it or not, acknowledge it or not, discuss it or not. It hovers over you, it follows you. It is up to us, however, whether we try to confront it or hide from it.

"I felt so much for them, the burden of such a childhood," Wiesel said to me. "To come home and see his parents, and the silence of the parents, and the pain, the frustrated pain he faces. Not easy for a child."

And not easy to comprehend. Often, before my mother would take up her nighttime position in the darkened living room of our Skokie home, she would drink hot black coffee at the kitchen table, long after my father had gone to sleep. Because the kitchen bordered my bedroom, I'd sometimes slide to the edge of the bed in the dark, open the door a crack and peek out at my mother, watching her sitting silently at the table. I didn't understand why, as my mother read a newspaper or magazine, her body trembled, a quaver constantly coursing through her hands and head, stillness eluding her.

Why was she like this? Why did she stay up when everyone had gone to bed? What was this all about? It was unfathomable to me at age ten and for years after, and I certainly never connected it to the most obvious source of all, the consequences of war.

In Wiesel, I found someone who understood my confusion.

"It's not easy to have such an existence," he said, referring to all the sons and daughters of the survivors. "Some children don't know what to do with it. Should they ask their parents? Should they not say anything? What is good for the parents? They don't know."

How do you ask your mother or father about what happened? How do you ask them to revisit losses they have been struggling to cope with ever since? How do you ask them to tell you about the worst nightmare imaginable? How do you even broach the subject? And how do you contend with the answer, should you get one?

It's all too much. And, of course, it's exponentially more so for the survivors than for their children. For on the other side of the silence between parents and children were experiences that the survivors could not really put into words. No one could, Wiesel believes.

"How does one tell this story?" he asked me. "Where do you begin? Is it before the ghetto? Is it in the ghetto? Where do you begin? And where do you end? Does it end really at liberation day? The topic to this day, so many years, so many decades later, it is still a kind of mystery, a mystery of mysteries. And you don't know how to touch it. The tragedy is the realization that some of us have that really only those who were there know what it meant to be there. Nobody else. Thank God.

"But at what point does a father tell his children?" continued Wiesel. "Come on. At what point? What is the age? Eight, nine, ten, eleven, twelve, fifteen? There is no age, recommendable age, to say that is the time to talk.

"When I was at *Yedioth Ahronoth*," he continued, referring to the Israeli newspaper where he'd worked more than half a century earlier, "I was still the UN correspondent there. There was an Italian correspondent—actually he was sent to Auschwitz, and he converted. A Jew converted! And he told me, 'I don't want my children even to know what I went through.'"

As if it were even possible to disguise it. As if the aftereffects of what happened wouldn't seep through in some manner.

In our house, even though I knew almost nothing of my parents' experiences, I already knew as a child the anger and thunder my father could unleash, the hysteria my mother could reach if provoked (often, unwittingly, by me). I simply didn't realize for a long time that the two were related, that virtually all the drama in our family ultimately stemmed from what both my parents had experienced but not discussed with us.

In retrospect, it seems as if almost all the trouble in our house originated in Eastern Europe, a lifetime ago.

My thoughts are echoed—or perhaps I should say predated—by the words of Wiesel's protagonist in *The Fifth Son*. A child of survivors, the character is tormented by his knowledge, and by his lack of knowledge, of what happened.

"Born after the war," he says, "I endure its effects. The children of survivors are almost as traumatized as the survivors themselves. I suffer from an Event I have not even experienced."

I realize now that, for the most part, I tried to navigate the tempests and traumas in our house by avoiding their source, steering clear of anything having to do with the Holocaust. When I overheard my aunts and uncles—also survivors—railing about it, I tuned out. This was unfortunate.

But Wiesel interpreted this tendency toward avoidance differently than I do now. More generously, for sure.

"In French, there is a marvelous word: *pudeur*," he said. "This means a kind of polite respect, but spiritual and psychological respect, out of love. Meaning it's so profound, why say things that for them [the survivors], every word brings back who knows what?"

Surely this is a kinder way of looking at our reluctance to ask our parents about what happened to them when it was still possible—in my case, when my father was alive and my mother more closely in touch with reality. One way or another, though, a silence on the subject prevailed in the homes of most survivors. I say this not only from my experience and observation but from research on the subject as well.

"Although a few survivors chose to speak about their Holocaust experiences in public forums—before organizations or educational groups, for example—survivors' revelations to their children were usually fragmentary and occurred over many years," wrote Dr. Aaron Hass, himself a child of survivors, in his study *In the Shadow of the Holocaust: The Second Generation.*

"Rarely did a survivor sit a child down and impart a complete account of what had happened to him and his family. Rather, the same events, impression or encounters were related repeatedly, so that in fact very little of that period of the parent's life was truly told. The child's difficulty in remembering his parents' accounts is partly a result of the fragmentary nature of the content and the failure of the survivor to provide either a coherent history or a sufficient context to the events recounted."

Not that Hass or anyone is blaming the survivors for being unable to put unspeakable, anarchic, life-threatening, life-altering events into narrative form. The survivors had many reasons to avoid the subject.

"They feared your pain and perhaps even your judgment," Wiesel said in his keynote address at the First International Conference of Children of Holocaust Survivors in New York in 1984. "Parents would like their children to feel proud of them and confident in their strength. That is why they could not talk to you and, when they did, why they felt pathetic, incoherent, helpless."

Wiesel, too, had found himself struggling to address this subject in his own writings.

"I still am not sure whether I found the words—I am not sure," he said to me, returning to this theme often in our conversations.

Yet for all the difficulties survivors experienced in speaking of their pasts, the impact of the story was very much present in my family's house, and many others, even if the details were not. Fear and paranoia enveloped our lives.

One evening during my high school years, I lingered outside the Skokie Public Library after it closed, chatting with a friend for an hour. When I got home, I found a police squad car parked out front awaiting me. The officer escorted me to the house, where my parents—nearly hysterical that I was an hour late in coming home—yelled at me for the fright I had given them. But I did not yet understand the source of their fears or the ferocity of their reaction to my brief delay.

For I was as far removed from their history and pain as any son could be. Anxiety and dread drove my avoidance of the *H* word and everything it signified. Looking back on it, I often have felt that I turned to music as a teenager to escape the turbulence and discord in our house and in my family. For when I was pounding the piano in our cramped living room, I couldn't hear them yelling at each other on the telephone. Music was my way out.

But I mustn't forget one other essential ingredient in the angst of my family and many others: guilt. The older I became, the worse I felt about what had happened to my parents and what they had lost: their parents and siblings, their youth and their dreams.

My father often said he had yearned to become a conductor; his musical gifts were apparent when he sang prayers in synagogue, everyone turning around to see whose voice produced such a thrilling sound, he said. Instead, my father spent his adult life laboring in a bakery at ungodly hours, suffering through crushing heat there every summer, his back aching from his war wounds all the while. My mother never even said what her dreams had been. And I never asked.

Guilt.

At least I'm not alone.

Family "situations that are unsolvable or difficult to remedy might instigate chronic guilt," wrote Drs. Miri Scharf and Ofra Mayseless in one of the most comprehensive recent psychological studies, "Disorganizing Experiences in Second- and Third-Generation Holocaust Survivors." "When children feel responsible for their parents' welfare (especially when seeing them miserable and unsatisfied), they might chronically feel that they have not done enough for their parents, and depressed people are particularly likely to engender chronic guilt in their offspring."

Others observed this phenomenon as well.

"The children openly talked about guilt as a pervasive element covering many aspects of their relationships with their parents," observed Cipora Katz and Franklin Keleman in their study "The Children of Holocaust Survivors: Issues of Separation" in the *Journal of Jewish Communal Service*. "Fantasies of separation or real attempts to separate from the family often evoked powerful guilt feelings, since the implicit loyalties would be violated."

And Dr. Hass pointed out that "guilt is a recurring theme in the literature describing children of survivors. Some offspring identify with their guilt-ridden parents. Others may experience a need to share in the past suffering of their parents and murdered family."

Given such histories, how is it possible for a person with any conscience *not* to feel guilty?

To my surprise, Wiesel rejected the idea. Completely.

"I don't want them to feel guilty," he said of children of survivors. "I don't want their parents to feel guilty. The *guilt feelings* really was an invented word that came from psychiatrists immediately after the war. The next generations should never feel guilty. What did they do?

"I know myself, I have done nothing in camp in order to survive. I was too timid and too weak. I have never done anything to survive. Usually when they distributed the soup, for instance, the others began pushing. I have never done it. I was afraid to be beaten up.

"I wanted to survive only because of my father. I knew if I die, he will die. But the moment he died in Buchenwald, if you read, go back to *Night* and see, between January 27 and April 11—he died January 27 or 8—I didn't live the rest of my life.

"So I didn't do anything to survive. Why should I feel guilty? Guilt feelings? No. Sadness, yes. But guilt? What guilt? The guilty should feel guilty."

Yet Wiesel acknowledged that for us, the second generation, a kind of deep regret, at least, seems natural. Clearly we are not responsible for what happened to our parents, but we hurt for what they endured. If we don't wish to call our pain guilt, we certainly can say we feel sorrow for what others did to them and for what we cannot repair.

As they reach the end of their days, our pain only increases.

The children of survivors "know that once their father dies, another chapter is being closed—who knows how many other chapters were closed?" said Wiesel. The anguish "is there. Maybe the son said, 'We didn't love them enough. We didn't give enough time for them. We didn't do enough to make his life or her life pleasurable or happy. And maybe we didn't allow him or permit him or ask him to write, to speak more about his experiences. Maybe he's taking his true story with him to the grave.'"

But while Wiesel acknowledged the dark sentiments we children of survivors feel, he offered a wholly different way of looking at them. He not only believed that guilt has no place in this equation, but he saw a completely different dynamic at work here: a role reversal in which the survivor parent needs protection, and the child oddly finds himself or herself attempting to provide it. To Wiesel, that's what was really happening here: children taking responsibility—emotional and other-wise—for the situation they and their parents are in.

"In a strange way, the child becomes the parents' parent," he told me.

In other words, the child tries to protect the parent from the after-effects of a tragedy that's difficult to discuss yet impossible to escape. The subject is always there, even before the child is born and ever after, even if it's barely spoken of. And though it's the parent who endured the Holocaust, the children often feel keenly responsible for the par-ents' suffering. Perhaps not out of guilt that is undeserved but out of responsibility that is commendable.

"They know more than the parents," said Wiesel of the children of survivors, a statement that confused me.

How could we possibly know more than our survivor parents?

"This was true during the Experience, as well," Wiesel went on to explain. "The young people, even teenagers, had to take care of their parents. It's not natural. It is the parents—the father, the mother—who take care of the children.

"But during those days and nights, somehow the child knew more—how to get around, how to get about, to go about things. I think I mention it, almost in passing, in *Night*, that my father and I, we didn't know what to counsel one another, what to do. And that was one of the worst things. That all of a sudden, my father didn't know how to be a father."

The same awkward role reversal, Wiesel contended, applies between survivors and their children today. The child tries to manage suffering he or she has not personally experienced and cannot fully grasp. This unusual thesis of Wiesel's is echoed in psychological research.

"The third theme that we identified as appearing to have disorganizing effects on the children [of survivors] reflects their strong need to please the parent, take care of the parent and assume responsibility for the parent's well-being," wrote Drs. Scharf and Mayseless.

"These needs could be manifested in a strong sense of commitment to obey the parent and/or strong role reversal, but the major issue was the children's sense of compulsion to act or feel this way without a way to express their autonomous wishes. Thus, the children felt coerced into this role, and did not assume it by choice. Role reversal refers to children's forfeiture of their own need for comfort, protection, and guidance so as to fulfill the parents' needs to an extent that exceeds the developmental norms in the culture."

At this point I must acknowledge that as soon as I told Wiesel about research that supports his observations and mine, he rejected it. When I cited the studies I'd immersed myself in, he questioned their methods, their results, even the very notion that it was possible to make scientific deductions or broad generalizations about how survivors and their families behaved and why. Time after time I would cite this study or that, and time after time he would point out flaws.

When I presented data that had been gathered and easily had persuaded me, he would respond, "It's difficult to say, because not all young people actually are part of this research, I'm sure. Let's say Brooklyn. Brooklyn had a huge percentage of Holocaust survivors, many Hasidic. I can tell you the researchers, those who did the statistics, did not call those families. First of all, Hasidic survivors didn't have telephones. Therefore, there's a huge omission. There must have been at least one hundred thousand survivors in Brooklyn. Their language was Yiddish. They didn't speak anything else. They and their children and their grandchildren spoke Yiddish. In school, at home, in yeshiva."

Wiesel's point being that the interviewers and data gatherers missed too many people, did not all speak Yiddish and therefore could not possibly have gathered representative data. Undeterred, I cited various surveys reporting how the second generation behaved.

Wiesel was consistently unconvinced. "I don't know, I didn't do the research," he would say. "It can be true, but not always. Not always."

And again later: "I worry about generalizations. Some people yes, others no."

Finally he became mildly exasperated with my unending data. "Don't generalize!" he said. "It depends."

Maybe he's right. Maybe each family's tragedy is different, and each child's response to it is therefore unlike any other. Maybe these scenarios cannot be scientifically documented.

But each one of us is, at the very least, an authority on what happened in our own homes. And in mine, I have come to believe that psychic pain was ubiquitous, manifesting itself in often strange and haunting ways.

"Can you imagine that anything could eliminate that pain?" Wiesel asked me.

He refused, however, to view anguish in a vacuum.

"But together with pain was happiness. Survivors have greater joy and greater despair," he said, and I had to admit that this was true.

I remember the excitement in our house when my father came home from work around two or three every afternoon, his arms cradling waxed bags overflowing with aromatic, freshly baked breads and pastries for us. We would begin to devour them at the kitchen table moments after he arrived, and he'd regale my mother with stories of what happened in the bakery that day: who marveled at his work and begged him for his recipe (to no avail); who took a swing at him in the rough-and-tumble of the bakery but quickly came to regret it. There was some joy in our house.

After we greeted my father and his bounty, he would take his customary nap. When he woke up, he began preparing dinner with my mother, whirling around the kitchen, grabbing pots and pans, tossing this spice or that one into the dish, transforming the rudimentary dinner he had taught my mother to make via his own baker's gifts and training.

On Sundays, he made matzo brei for us for breakfast, Yiddish music playing over the radio on the *Jewish Community Hour* program. Sometimes, when he was in a very good mood, my father would take out his ivory-colored Hohner accordion, the one he had bought after the war while recuperating in Wiesbaden, Germany. He would play by ear tunes he remembered from the Old Country. Occasionally he would whistle along, and in those moments, I knew he was back there, remembering his life before it unraveled, and immediately after.

There was indeed happiness in our house, but it was laced with sorrow and rage, our family's traumas waiting patiently to fully bloom. The death of my father at age sixty-nine, in 1991, left my mother alone again for the first time in roughly forty years, and that is, I believe, when her long-festering fears began to metastasize.

Unfortunately in my lack of awareness of what really was happening in our house, I had done nothing all my life to help my mother or to prevent this disaster. I was a mere observer, and not a very astute one, doing nothing to ease my parents' pain.

Surprisingly, though, Wiesel said the opposite was true. Children of survivors, like me, "didn't know how to help, but they did," he insisted. "I know some survivors, really, were saved by their children's joy, by their children's hope, by their children's passion. They were helped by their children. Simply by being. Just being."

Yes, that much at least I had done. Though not much more. I was there. If this helped my parents, I'm grateful. But the truth at the core of our family's troubles was too potent to touch.

3

A Burden and Privilege

We were born into a complex and difficult history, cryptically disclosed in fragments by those survivors who chose to say something to their children and in silence by those who did not. We witnessed parental behaviors that seemed peculiar at the time but were quite natural, in a way, considering the context.

In light of all this, I believe we sons and daughters of survivors carry conflicting emotions embedded in Holocaust families and perhaps unfamiliar to those who have not been affected directly by that event. We cannot necessarily even put into words how we feel about a subject barely articulated in our homes as we were growing up. We may feel responsible but inadequate, aware yet unaware. As a second-generation friend of mine has put it to me more than once, "We knew, and we didn't know."

What are we children of survivors to do with all of this?

"To accept the heritage, which can be a very heavy heritage, left by their parents, first of all," said Wiesel. "To accept it, without giving the parents a guilt feeling and without allowing them to feel that maybe they failed. Which means to protect their parents, protect their parents' memories, protect their parents' lives, to protect their parents' dreams, to protect them. It's a very heavy responsibility."

But how could anyone live up to such an obligation? How can anyone do justice to all this? If it has taken me the majority of my life simply to discern what really was happening in our house more than half a century ago, how could I possibly fulfill this responsibility at this late date? How can you make up for such a long period of neglect? What am I—and the other children and grandchildren and great-grandchildren of survivors—supposed to do?

"Just to be," said Wiesel. "Be authentically you. Meaning that you are not here having just come down from heaven ready-made, without a past and without any personal identity. You came here as children of those who were there with the legacy, with the history. And try to understand why the parents at one point stopped talking, why the parents can't really talk, why the parents avoid certain subjects, and why they come back to this.

"First of all, understand the parents. Understand what the second generation means for their parents. What children mean for their parents. That they are the only source of joy, the only source of hope, the only source of pleasure, the real source of meaning—everything.

"The closer we are to the event, which is behind us," added Wiesel, "the more the obligation to at least make it part of our future, of our vision of the future."

Yet the subject and its responsibilities remain overwhelming. And Wiesel did not seem to be saying what the second generation is supposed to do. So I asked him again.

"I don't think that the second generation has to do anything except what they are doing," he answered, clearly declining to give me—or anyone else—specific instructions on how to live.

"No one has the right to give them lessons. No one has the right to say, 'Behave that way, because this is what we expect.' No one has that right. But they themselves choose what to do."

My choice came late: to write my mother's story. I did so not as a first option but as a last resort, when it was clear there was nothing more anyone could do for my mother but keep her safe. For she refused to speak to psychiatrists or any medical professionals, whom she regards as the enemy to this day, and refused to take medicines in the belief that everyone is trying to kill her (as indeed nearly everyone once was).

"When people have tremendous trauma, like your mother, they simply never forget," Dr. David Rosenberg, the psychiatrist who diagnosed her post-traumatic stress disorder, told me. "She is in the thrall of old memories and old defenses."

Thus the well-dressed, impeccably coiffed woman who entered the nursing home in 2001 refused to accept any of the new clothes and shoes I brought her, eventually wearing fraying skirts and tattered blouses. She began to look like someone who was on the run, which she indeed believed herself to be.

There was nothing left for me to do but write. I'd come late to my parents' story, but because of what happened to my mother, I was finally catapulted into it.

As always, Wiesel saw the positive, hopeful side of this belated awareness. "I know some people who were detached totally from the past," he said, referring to second-generation children perhaps even more alienated from their parents' histories than I was.

"'Parents, please, stop,'" Wiesel said, taking on the voice of a child of survivors. "'You suffered, we are with you, and we love you. Stop. Just stop.'

"It happened this way in some cases, very few," Wiesel added. "I don't think it works. It's not natural. But you could say, 'Could that be a solution? Is there a solution?' I don't know.

"But I turned it around," he continued, choosing to focus not on those who turn away from their parents' stories but on those who embrace them.

"I find beauty in it," he said. "I find hope in it. I find exuberance in it, passion in it. Our children, instead of saying, 'Look, your generation suffered, it's enough, turn the page, close the page, finished'—they got involved. More involved, more than I even thought they could.

"The children of survivors that I had in my classes—extraordinary. Also, because of that Event, they take up all kinds of causes, humanized causes. But not only for Jews, but for other people.

"I try to say to them, 'We are first Jewish, remember that. But nevertheless, as a Jew, you must look beyond.'

"What I try to do, as the Jew in me is universal: don't neglect all the other sides. Only Jewish? No! The Jew in you must be interested in who is not Jewish. And you know, very few children of survivors have disappointed me or their parents.

"They pick up the pieces of the story," Wiesel added. "Now it's not only the sons and the daughters, but also the grandchildren pick up the story."

Some more than others. If carrying the story forward represents a worthy response, I'm glad for that, though it seems a small contribution.

Still, I do wonder: What if my mother had not had such an extreme, dramatic reaction to her Holocaust past? What if she had not run out of her house, had not been picked up twice in a row by the police, had not maintained—as she does to this day—that there is a yellow Star of David on her clothes? Would I then have pursued her story so rigorously?

And even if I had decided to try to understand what happened to my parents, would I have been able to spend so much time and effort pursuing the story if I weren't a journalist positioned to do so? What if I hadn't become a writer? What if I had become a pianist? What would I have done then?

I posed this question at a medical conference to Dr. Alessandra Scalmati, a psychiatrist who has treated Holocaust survivors and their children for years. Her answer silenced my doubts, at least for a while.

"Why do you think you became a journalist?" she said.

Why indeed? Was the story I avoided while growing up the very reason I became a writer—eventually to tell it? Surely I didn't consciously realize that the most important story I would ever write would be the one that happened right before me, in my family's house.

Yet once I began working on it, I came to feel fortunate, in an odd way, to be doing so. At last I could puncture the silence. Belatedly I could take up the responsibility of telling a sacred tale.

Wiesel saw the value in such a quest, no matter who pursues it.

"Look, I am not a child of survivors—my parents didn't survive," he said. "But we are a generation of survivors, we are children of a generation of survivors. Therefore, I call it a privileged generation. What this generation hears and repeats and remembers is unlike any other. No other generation had that privilege—and that difficulty. It's a legacy almost in the mystical sense. It means you are endowed with a mission. And we say to the students, 'Now go and do something with it.'"

That is the challenge, isn't it? Clearly everyone must discover what to do with this legacy. There's no universal answer—that much I gathered from my discussions with Wiesel. Though it was obvious by now that Wiesel wasn't going to tell me specifically how we children of survivors should conduct our lives, he took another approach, suggesting instead what we shouldn't do.

"The mission is surely *not* to keep quiet and do nothing and let history unfold itself again and the killer sleep well," he said.

"That's not the mission. Whatever the meaning is, that is not the meaning."

Still, I sought specifics from Wiesel on what the second generation ought to do. I started with the most obvious issue: the fundamental act of having children.

Understandably survivors yearned for grandchildren, and many lived to enjoy this miracle, to see life emerging where once death had prevailed. I did not make this possible for my parents. So what about those of us in the second generation who will not give rise to subsequent generations? Who will now ensure that our parents' heroism will be honored through other lives? Was it our duty to have children? Did we fail?

"There it is either because of a choice or because they can't have children," said Wiesel. "We have to be very sensitive to it. We cannot hurt anyone. We shouldn't. Some people couldn't have children. I've known them. Then what? What do they do?"

"Well, that means, in those circumstances, their books are their children," said Wiesel, perhaps tailoring his response to the second-generation son, and writer, sitting next to him. Which I appreciated.

"Their stories are their children," added Wiesel. "They write about it, and therefore they compensate, and they know it."

In effect, Wiesel seemed to be saying that having children is not the only way to fulfill one's obligations as a child of survivors. That there are many paths to take.

"Oh, absolutely more than one," said Wiesel. "What is clear is what the mission is: the mission is to continue. That surely is the mission. Why? Because the opposite is also clear: To let the killer get away with these crimes and without anyone knowing about it? No.

"The children receive the story from their parents. And they believe it's their mission now to do something with these stories. It's clear. At least that we know. Since they were there and they inherited the stories, they must do something with the stories.

"One task is almost the easiest one: to prevent the deniers from writing their history the way they see it. Because surely there are already deniers, and there will be more. And one day they'll dominate the scene. They will say, 'It's not true, come on. Because it couldn't be true.'

"And therefore, that is now the task, the mission of the children to say, 'Ha! We heard it from the best witnesses available to us: my father, my mother.' That gives weight."

Yes, indeed, that weight is considerable. And it can be felt by all of us children of survivors, I told Wiesel. The gravity of the story and the implications of so much suffering can be seen in the struggles of our parents. We witnessed their insomnia, their financial challenges, the chronic pain of their losses.

We felt all of this.

"It isn't easy," acknowledged Wiesel, brooking no self-pity from any heir to this legacy. "It shouldn't be easy. Look: It's not entertaining. And you, as a journalist, you know very well that if it's not entertaining, it doesn't sell. If it doesn't sell, that means the publisher won't publish, it means the newspapers won't publish.

"But because it doesn't sell, and because you are still here, that is why your voice must be heard, and continue to be heard, through history."

I believe Wiesel meant that precisely because this story is such a difficult one, precisely because some people now invoke the phrase *Holocaust fatigue*, we children of survivors should labor that much harder to make ourselves heard. Precisely because there is resistance, our determination should be that much greater.

Furthermore, we must bear up under the weight of our families' autobiographies, Wiesel seemed to be saying. Any burden that we experience obviously is slight compared to what our parents carried. Any pushback that we encounter is minor compared to what our parents confronted.

Wiesel insisted that our voices be heard. That was as close as I could get to eliciting from him some guidance on how the children of survivors should consider proceeding.

It was good advice, and he would expand upon it.

4

We Are All Witnesses

As I considered Wiesel's comments, I concluded that, to him, it all came down, in a way, to a single word that he repeated often through our conversations: *witness*. Whether we have children or not, whether we are writers or not, whether we are able to publish or not, we sons and daughters of survivors are quite literally born to be witnesses to what happened—even though, in most instances, the events we are to witness happened long before we were born.

"The witness prevails," Wiesel said to me often.

I asked him to explain.

"The role of the witness is actually a religious precept," he said. "God says to the Jewish people, 'You are my witnesses, for I am the Lord.' Therefore, my generation is a generation of witnesses. But then I have written: To listen to a witness is to become a witness."

Wiesel's religiously infused definition of a witness went far beyond and far deeper than *Webster's* dictionary description of "a person who saw, or can give a firsthand account of, something." To Wiesel, all of us in the second generation are witnesses, and everyone who listens to a survivor or to their children becomes one. Moreover, to be a witness is a sacred duty and privilege, he was saying. A witness is not merely a passive observer of what happened but, in a way, the eyes and ears of a higher power, according to Wiesel's view.

In the case of children of survivors, we have witnessed close up the aftereffects of the Holocaust, the damage that was done to our parents, the stories they did or did not explicitly tell us. But we've also witnessed their heroism in managing to press on afterward. We are the living, breathing repositories of their life stories, inasmuch as we could ascertain or sense their autobiographies. We are the witnesses who convey their tragedies and triumphs to the future.

In so doing, we "honor their memory," said Wiesel. "And I use the word *honor* advisedly. There is honor in that. Because in the beginning, they were all embarrassed to be survivors, as if they had done something wrong."

Indeed, there was much shame associated with being a survivor immediately after the Holocaust and long after. Even in Israel—before the trial of Adolph Eichmann in 1961—survivors were considered something close to pariahs.

"It doesn't seem possible," Wiesel wrote in his first volume of memoirs, *All Rivers Run to the Sea*, "but at school pupils called their immigrant classmates *sabonim*, little 'soap cakes.'" This was a macabre reference to Nazis using parts of dead Jewish bodies for ignoble purposes.

Around the world, the survivors often were considered pitiful and pitiable, before Wiesel and others showed humanity how to think of them in another, more aptly heroic light. Continuing this mission is our job as witnesses, Wiesel was saying. And if our parents are still living, we should share what we have witnessed even with them. Especially with them.

"You should say, 'Dear parents, you represent the honor of the world, the honor of humanity, the honor of God. Not those who diminished you, surely no,'" Wiesel told me. "But this has to be said forcefully."

Furthermore, we need to express this reverence sooner rather than later, Wiesel insisted.

"Don't wait—just don't wait," he said. "They don't have time. Don't wait. Which means whatever you do now must have a sense of urgency. None of us is immortal. So don't wait."

Being a witness to my family's story came quite naturally—if very belatedly—to me, for a year after my mother ran out of her house and was diagnosed with PTSD, I began to write and then speak publicly on the subject. But, like many of my peers, I was a witness at a vast distance. The world I lived in, modern-day urban America, was about as far removed from my parents' Eastern European origins as was imaginable. And that remains true of my friends and contemporaries, our connection to the Judaism that our forebears died for becoming tenuous, according to research.

A survey on Jewish life in America released by the Pew Research Center's Religion & Public Life project on October 1, 2013—the first such study in ten years—found that while 94 percent of US Jews "say they are proud to be Jewish," there has been a dramatic rise in Jews marrying outside the religion and not raising their children to be Jewish. Intermarriage hit a new high of 58 percent for all Jews, compared to 17 percent before 1970.

In analyzing Jews who practice religion and those who have "no religion" but identify with Judaism via culture or ethnicity, the survey found that "more than 90 percent of Jews by religion who are currently raising minor children in their home say they are raising those children Jewish or partially Jewish. In stark contrast, the survey finds that two thirds of Jews of no religion say they are not raising their children Jewish or partially Jewish."

Meanwhile, only 31 percent of adult Jews belong to a synagogue, and 32 percent had a Christmas tree at home in 2012 (71 percent of intermarried Jews put up the tree).

All of which led me to a difficult but inescapable question: After all our parents suffered and lost for being Jews, are we turning our backs on their faith and values and those of our ancestors? Is assimilation achieving what historic tragedy could not?

"Assimilation is not a new trend," said Wiesel, more sanguine on the subject than I expected. "We always faced it. Assimilation to Communism. Assimilation to all kinds of ideologies. It's not new. We survived all that. I'm not worried. I know some people are. I am not. We survived almost three thousand years. We can survive more.

"There have always been assimilated Jews. But then they come back. Theodor Herzl," continued Wiesel, referring to the father of modern

Zionism, "came from an assimilated family. And he was the one who created a Jewish state.

"I am not worried about that. I think it's the wrong option for a Jew, naturally. Some Jews chose it. After the war, there were some Jews who became—because of the war—assimilated. And others became more religious—for the same reason," meaning the events of the Holocaust.

We may worry about whether we are measuring up to our unspoken duties as the children of survivors and the witnesses of their travails. We may question whether we are becoming so far removed from our parents' stories and ways of life that our traditions are becoming more historical than fully lived. But Wiesel was not worried. On the contrary, he said he was encouraged by what he saw from the second generation.

Considering our backgrounds, he said, the children of survivors easily could have become adversaries of society. But instead they chose to become its allies, he said, a point echoed in research.

Dr. Elissa Ganz showed in her study "Intergenerational Transmission of Trauma: Grandchildren of Holocaust Survivors" that even 3Gs (the third generation), as often has been noted of 2Gs (the second generation), are twice as likely as their counterparts to choose what might generally be called helping professions: medicine, psychology, social work, and the like.

Perhaps they are trying to save the world from events that happened before they were born.

"Well, subconsciously," said Wiesel. "I don't think that they chose that simply to show the world. It was subconscious. But it was logically the right thing to do."

On the other hand, added Wiesel, "If they had done something terribly wrong, I can imagine the speech I would have made if I were a lawyer: 'Look, how could they not, when they had to live with their parents, who went through Auschwitz and Buchenwald and so forth?'"

Instead, said Wiesel, the survivors' children often picked up their parents' concerns, fighting anti-Semitism and experiencing a righteous rage over what happened.

"The children of survivors, they feel the anger—for us," said Wiesel. "The second generation thinks: 'The world was made by our parents. So now we ask, What did they do to our parents?'"

To answer this question, and others, many of us in the second generation sooner or later make a kind of pilgrimage to the places where our parents were born and their families massacred. In so doing, we deepen our role as witnesses.

Continuously I encounter articles, books, lectures, and documentary films made by sons and daughters who felt compelled to go to where the killings occurred. I was among them. The second generation has made its way to what remains of the camps, to the blood-soaked earth of Central and Eastern Europe to see the decimated villages, to walk on soil that, as in my mother's town of Dubno, amounts to a sprawling, unmarked burial ground. To see who lives there now. To tell them what happened. To show them that we are still here.

"That's human," said Wiesel, in assessing the journeys we children of survivors take to ancestral places.

"Our sages tell us there are certain questions that are being posed to human beings. The first one is, Where do you come from? You should know where you come from. Second, you should know where you are going. And the third is you should also know whom you are going to face, ultimately, to give an account of your life.

"But the first is, Where do you come from? Therefore, if part of me remained in Sighet, it's because I come from Sighet. So I speak much more about my youth in Sighet than about my youth in Auschwitz. That's because I believe that Auschwitz belongs to the unspeakable world, the unspeakable terms. There are no words for it.

"It was a kind of universe," Wiesel added. "A different universe. They [Nazis] saw their creation alongside God's Creation. One created by God and the other one by man."

And yet we children and grandchildren of survivors go to these hellish places. Why? It seems to be a kind of compulsion.

"They want to go back to the place where their parents were children," said Wiesel. "That means something to them. And when they go back to their parents afterward, they ask them all the essential questions. They ask, 'Tell us. How was it?'"

Like me, I suppose, the other travelers of my generation need to see these places in order to make them real. The neurologist who treats my lifelong migraine headaches insists that even if my mother hadn't run out of her house that frozen night in February 2001, I eventually would have traveled to her dying village anyway. I would have been compelled to go.

"Yeah, yeah, absolutely," said Wiesel. "There is an urge, an irresistible urge. But not only to go—to go with their parents. They go alone too. But to be there with their parents. And for them, it's a kind of justice: 'You think that you got rid of us? Here we are—with our children.'

"Surely not an easy experience to go back to those places," added Wiesel. "You know why—because and because and because. At the same time, there is something in us that draws us to these places, to be there.

"When I went back to my little town, Sighet, I remember the last exodus, which means the day really we left, in 1944. Which means you relive the event that will mark your life. So on one hand, everything in you wants to forget, because it was really humiliation. To be rejected by everybody in that town that were your neighbors—total rejection.

"And yet you go back, you want to live it again. And you hope, therefore, that by being there again, as free Jews, free men, you redeem history.

"Twelve thousand Jews lived in Sighet—maybe there are over fifty there now," he added. "Is it a real return? You go to a cemetery. You go from cemetery to cemetery.

"And, nevertheless, you cannot not go."

Having taken such an odyssey, I—like uncounted others—have made contact with my mother's terrifying past. There was no other way.

"I think that is the role of the survivors' children today," said Wiesel. "To come closer to their parents. And in order for the children to know who they are, they must know who they [the parents] were as children."

In this way, we strive to serve as witnesses to their lives and their stories.

And, perhaps, as Wiesel said, we nurture new witnesses by speaking of what we saw.

5

The Untouchable Past

For children of survivors, making contact with our parents' pasts and their core identities can be daunting. My father, in his apparent desire to project strength and stoicism, allowed my sister and me no window of intimacy or hint of vulnerability. Only once did I see him shed a tear, at the funeral of a beloved brother-in-law—also a survivor—only to wipe it quickly away.

I cannot remember once looking my father in the eye for more than a moment or two, unless it was to see his anger flashing at me for some transgression I had committed.

Perhaps Dr. Joel Sadavoy, head of geriatric psychiatry at Mount Sinai Hospital in Toronto, was right when he wrote that many survivors invented "what may be termed a traumatically induced 'false self.'" By this, Dr. Sadavoy meant "a form of character armor, protecting the victim's vulnerable true self that was impinged upon by the trauma."

I never got past that protective armor surrounding my father's psyche. My mother, too, revealed little of her pain and loss, except through the unusual behaviors I decoded much later in life. It was as if there had been a wall around each of my parents, preventing anyone—or at least me—from seeing past the strong, brave fronts they presented.

I did not know how to get through that impenetrable exterior, and I don't know if I ever really wanted to, until it was too late.

"That's why so many children of survivors, they don't go that far, because they were afraid of the price," said Wiesel.

I wasn't sure what he meant.

"They were afraid of the price because their parents were afraid of the price," he continued.

"What it means?" said Wiesel, perhaps recognizing the confusion on my face.

"Ultimately did it mean, if I want to live, it's at the expense of someone else?" he asked, referencing his time in Auschwitz and Buchenwald.

"If the Germans had, let's say, a quota, they had to clear one hundred people, then so those who survived there should feel guilty because they were not chosen? It's absurd. But even an absurd reality has a certain weight.

"And so the children of survivors sometimes are afraid to go to the end of the quest. At the same time, they are intrigued. They want to go to the end, to come closer to their parents. And the parents are afraid that they came too close. And all they want is to protect their children."

In his own way, I believe Wiesel was trying to illuminate the gulf or space that I—and surely other children of survivors—felt separating myself from my parents and their pasts. What I saw as a wall surrounding my mother and father Wiesel viewed as a fear on behalf of both generations to get too close to the untouchable truth.

There are secrets in our parents' stories, things that happened that we never could understand and that our parents are trying to shield us from. We can get only as close as they will allow and as near as we dare. We are kept away by their fears and ours.

But our parents are not the only ones who often seem far outside our reach. For many of us, the generation preceding our parents was absent. When I was a child, I often wondered why everyone on TV had a grandfather or grandmother while I had neither. The answer eventually became apparent, but the painful void remained. I longed to have a grandparent to talk to, to be treasured by, just like on TV. But that loss never could be filled.

Wiesel acknowledged as much.

"I remember in my life, I was a child, and if I was very happy, I remember, I couldn't really talk to my parents about it, but I could speak to my grandfather," said Wiesel. "He lived nearby in a small village. I asked somebody to take me to him, I spent time with him. There's something about grandparents in relation to children that is irreplaceable."

So what are we to do with this gap? What do we do about these critically important people in our lives who are not merely missing but were murdered? What should we do about the stories that have not—could not—be told to us? How do we try to fill this emptiness and find these narratives?

"You reinvent them," said Wiesel. "First of all, use your parents or grandparents as long as they are still alive. Let them tell you stories. Write it down. They will feel grateful to you for doing what you are doing to keep their stories alive.

"Make it almost a kind of luxury for you, a luxury visit, that every week you come at least once, or every month you come once and take stories.

"Just say, 'Tell me a story. What was the first story you heard when you were a child? Tell me a story.'"

In essence, Wiesel was implying, we need to gather up what's left of the memories of our grandparents' lives. We may find it directly from them, if they survived, and from our parents as well. We can scour history books, too, to try to fill in the blanks and capture the stories of those who are missing.

"Fill in the details," he said. "Sure, they are gone, but they are here. They are gone physically, but not metaphysically."

Wiesel believed, in other words, that the sense and the feeling and the presence of vanished grandparents—and others—can be conjured up in a way. Not in the flesh but in the heart and mind. We can make contact, we can hear and inhabit the stories if we try to find them. And he offered specific ways to try to reclaim a stolen past, to get a sense of what came before, to feel what no longer can be touched.

"The best thing is to take one event—today, that day," he said, referring to an anniversary or another significant occasion. "Maybe the liquidation of the Warsaw ghetto, or the extinguishing of something.

That day is different. In Judaism today we call it the Day of Remembrance, Yom HaShoah. You can pick another day. Maybe a day when your grandparent died, and you make that day different. That day perhaps you read only poems written by those children who died. Some of the most dramatic and beautiful poems are written by youngsters, teenagers who perished. So beautiful it breaks your heart.

"There are no rules. Every family has its individual ways and every person has his own way," Wiesel continued. "The subject is so vast and so huge that you can do anything. Let's say you find in your distant family one person with whom you identify, and you decide you want to know more about that person. It can be a grandparent, an uncle, a great-grandparent: I want to know more about that person. And that in itself could become a good book later on!"

Wiesel held great faith in such a process, a kind of immersion into another time and place that somehow indeed puts us close to it. My journeys to Eastern Europe have proven to me that he was right. By standing in the streets my mother walked as a child, by going inside the home where she spent the few years of her innocence, I felt as if I were closer to her hidden childhood than I had imagined possible. I was surrounded by it. I was there.

At the same time, however, as much as we travel and interview and read and study, we have to acknowledge that we will never fully understand what happened to our parents and grandparents, who they were, what they would have meant to us and us to them. We were not with them. We cannot really know.

"How can you?" said Wiesel, as if recognizing the limits of even his hopeful view of trying to grasp the elusive past. "So, therefore, you must accept with humility the limitations. This is something on which I must quote myself: 'Only those who were there know what it meant to be there. Others will never know.'"

And so we, the second generation, accept the boundaries of our quest, even as we pursue it. Many of us will never know what it means to call someone "grandma" or "grandpa" or who those people were. Yet in his apparently innate hopefulness, Wiesel contended that the second generation can turn even this emptiness into something positive.

"You wake up in the morning, and you have a surplus of love, which could have been destined for the grandparents," he said. "Don't waste it. Use it for your parents, for your children, for other survivors, for the world. Not only for the Jewish people, but for the world. This is an unused surplus. Use it up helping others, understanding others, living with others."

One tack that some grandchildren of survivors have been taking, however, seems amiss to me. Some have been getting their forearms tattooed with the same numbers that had been branded onto their grandparents' forearms in Auschwitz. Clearly this has noble intentions: honoring the legacy of families by wearing the very numerals that sentenced Jews to probable death. Now the grandchildren take ownership of those numbers, as if to turn the tables on the persecutors and wear the tattoo. It becomes a gesture of solidarity, defiance, continuity, and affirmation of life: for only those who lived could have passed these numbers on.

Yet it seems a little too easy to me, too glib. How simple to walk into a tattoo parlor and have a few numerals etched into your arm—without enduring the mortal fears and deprivations that those numbers signified to the people forced to wear them. The grandchildren have not paid the price that came with these numbers, and therefore, in my view, may not have a moral right to brandish them.

I asked Wiesel what he thought about this.

"I read about it—what can I say?" said Wiesel. "I don't know. If they feel that's the way. I don't know. We come from a tradition that doesn't believe in that. We believe in writing. These children could write their own books, as children of children of survivors. Which for us is the way: the modus operandi is to write.

"But, nevertheless, who am I to tell them what to do or not to do? If they feel that's the way for them, go ahead."

Perhaps Wiesel's view was better than mine. Certainly more generous. Even if no one today has earned the right to wear those fraught numbers, perhaps I have no right to dismiss the practice either. Each of us must decide for ourselves—or at least that's what Wiesel contended.

In the end, though, surely it's better to focus on what we children and grandchildren of survivors share than what separates us. The survivors went through great sorrows to make our lives possible, not only during the Holocaust but after, when they had to survive anew in foreign lands, haunted by their memories.

Many, in fact, vowed not to bring children into an "ugly and evil world," as Wiesel put it to me. "I don't trust the world with my children," he remembered thinking in the aftermath of the war.

But survivors had children anyway, as a gesture of hope, Wiesel said. Then he told me the story of a survivor who lost her family and regularly visited the maternity wing of a Jewish hospital. She would ogle the babies, sometimes picking them up and saying, "Look, Hitler, we have another child."

To Wiesel, each Jewish child—each of us children of survivors—is a direct response to the millions of children killed.

As the generation of survivors slowly but inevitably disappears, the reverence that now is belatedly bestowed upon them "should also now pass on to the children of survivors," Wiesel said to me. "They, too, are in a special category. To be a child of survivors is to be miraculous. What had to be done for a child to be born! For the survivors to overcome fear."

And when the last survivor finally passes away, we will be the ones to speak for them, to carry their pasts forward. For this reason, among others, the children of survivors surely need each other.

"I'm for gatherings, for meetings—I love it, because people should be together," said Wiesel. "We are not alone. Man is not alone in the world. Especially when you have a common background. You have to compare notes, especially when you come out of such an excruciating experience. You may think that only you know. Others actually went through the same thing. So it is important."

When our parents and grandparents are gone, we will have only each other, the stories we have gathered, and a mission to share them.

6

Why Do They Hate Us?

I t took millennia for the enmity toward Jews to erupt into the Holocaust, leading all of us to ask simply, Why?

Why does this hatred stretch so far back in time and so far forward,
with anti-Semitism flourishing today, even after millions of Jews were
destroyed? Though perhaps it's foolish and futile to try to find a rational
underpinning for the tragic irrationality of the Holocaust, surely there's
no way of trying to understand what happened to our parents without
looking at the malice at the root of it all.

And so I asked Wiesel, Why?

For him, the pain of this bigotry began early, he told me, well before
the Holocaust, when he was a child.

"Summer it's raining, winter it's snowing, and anti-Semites are in the
street waiting for me," he recalled. "It was part of nature, so to speak.
Remember, in those years, in the thirties, with the Jewish community,
we could never, ever expect an evening without an anti-Semitic attack,
somehow, somewhere.

"Especially, let's say, during Christmas, we were supposed to pay
the price for Jesus's birth, and then in April for his death. For no matter what, there was always a reason for the anti-Semites to beat up a
Jew in the street.

"And I had *payot*," added Wiesel, referring to the long strands of
hair that Orthodox boys and men leave to dangle below their temples.

"And their pleasure was, somehow, to pull on my *payot*. Really, what kind of pleasure can that be? But they loved it."

At hearing these words, again I remembered something my father told me so many decades ago. As a youth walking through the streets of Sosnowiec, Poland, years before the war, my father was cornered by three strapping Poles. He knew a beating awaited him. Or at least he knew that's what the threesome intended for him.

My father said he grabbed something nearby—a rock? a piece of a pipe? I can't remember the details—and he smacked one of the three; the young man crumpled to the ground. When the other two rushed my father, he swung ferociously at them, bloodying them, and watched the threesome run off to torment another, weaker Jew another day.

I might have doubted this heroic tale but for the number of times my father told it to friends, relatives, and anyone else who asked him about life in the Old Country. This was not merely a story for my father: It was a defining moment in his life and a statement of principle, an affirmation of his determination to fight despite difficult odds—long before the Nazis made the odds impossible. It was my father's deeply held testimony, too, about the nature of anti-Semitism and how Jews in Poland were hated long before Hitler lit the fuse to so much rage.

I was moved that Wiesel was illuminating the subject of anti-Semitism in much the same way my father had, recalling through personal experience the bitter foreshadowing of the Holocaust.

"Why do they hate us? Why?" asked Wiesel. "So I know all the answers. In the beginning, it was religious reasons. Other times, it was social reasons. They hate us either because we are too rich or too poor, either because we are too ignorant or too learned, too successful or too failing. All the contradictions merge in the anti-Semite.

"And yet, one thing he knows: he hates Jews. He doesn't even know who Jews are. In general, I say, the anti-Semite—let *him* tell me why he hates me. Why should I answer for him?"

There can be no just explanation or rationale, of course, for any group hatred, so as I thought about it, I realized there was no answer to the question I'd asked Wiesel. And yet I felt compelled to continue inquiring about the how, why, and wherefore of this prejudice, just as Wiesel continuously grappled with these questions himself.

Anti-Semitism, Wiesel said to me, is "as old as the Jewish people. From the very beginning. Jewish people began where, in Egypt? They were slaves, hopefully good slaves, working very hard. Why would they hate us? There were so many other slaves, other nations, other religions. Why would they hate us already then?"

We don't know. Not really. The mythology of Jews killing Christ doesn't quite suffice to explain millennia of hatred culminating in mass murder, does it? What we know for sure is that this grievance thrives to this day, evidenced in ways sensational and mundane.

Everyone attuned to the news has seen coverage of the murder of Jews by Islamic terrorists in a kosher market in Paris in January 2015; the killing of four at the Jewish Museum in Brussels in May 2014; protestors shouting "death to Israel" at pro-Palestinian rallies in Belgium and France and "Gas the Jews!" at such events in Germany in the summer of 2014, after the latest war in Gaza.

Beneath these egregious events lies a more everyday brand of contempt. The largest survey ever commissioned by the Anti-Defamation League, released in May 2014, polled 53,100 individuals in 102 countries covering 96 languages and dialects. It found that 26 percent of those surveyed held "deeply" anti-Semitic views. Seventy percent of those identified as anti-Semitic said they never had met a Jew. Only 54 percent of respondents said they had heard of the Holocaust; two out of three said they either had not heard of the Holocaust or did not believe accounts of it to be accurate.

In effect, the Holocaust may as well have gone undetected for all the effect it had on humanity's subsequent regard for Jews (or lack of it).

To Wiesel, the pervasiveness and durability of anti-Semitism represented the antithesis of Jewish identity.

"What is the contribution of the Jewish people to history?" Wiesel asked, before offering an answer. "To emphasize the role of humanity—in the human being and in society.

"Which means I would put everywhere a question: And what about humanity? No one in Germany—all the scientists and philosophers and the highly educated—asked this simple question: What about humanity in all this? In Auschwitz? What about humanity?'

"They just did it and enjoyed it."

Perhaps nothing expresses the essence of humanity, and its most sublime achievements, more eloquently than music, a realm in which Jews long have flourished and the arena in which I have spent most of my life. Yet I learned long ago that even here anti-Semitism runs deep, a depressing reflection of the historic breadth of the hatred of Jews. Even in music you can see the essence of anti-Semitism and the groundwork for the Holocaust.

The musical genius Richard Wagner, who extended the harmonic possibilities of classical composition and the dramatic range of the operatic stage, was uninhibited in expressing his antipathy toward Jews in his writings. It was not mere coincidence that the Nazis embraced Wagner's music, making it the musical accompaniment to the Holocaust.

I find it impossible to listen to Wagner's work—which I do not go out of my way to encounter—without considering its brutal historical context and portents.

"I don't listen to him," said Wiesel, when I brought up the subject. "I know it's naive. After all, he died before the Holocaust began. Nevertheless, I'm entitled to certain naive decisions."

Or maybe not so naive. The associations of Wagner's music with Nazism are not happenstance, and it's possible to acknowledge Wagner's musical achievements while remembering his underlying philosophies and the uses to which his music not surprisingly was put. Wagner stated his case directly in his essay "Judaism in Music" in 1850, reissuing the screed in 1869.

"The Jew—who, as everyone knows, has a God all to himself—in ordinary life strikes us primarily by his outward appearance, which, no matter to what European nationality we belong, has something disagreeably foreign to that nationality: instinctively we wish to have nothing in common with a man who looks like that," wrote Wagner, in a single sentence branding Jews as outsiders, aliens, enemies. Among Wagner's objections were the cadences of Jewish speech, which he considered a "creaking, squeaking, buzzing snuffle."

Moreover, wrote Wagner, "Our whole European art and civilization, however, have remained to the Jew a foreign tongue."

To Wagner, as to all anti-Semites, Jews were different, not quite human, at least insofar as their ability to relate to the rest of humanity: "Never does the Jew excite himself in mutual interchange of feelings with us, but—so far as we are concerned—only in the altogether special egoistic interest of his vanity or profit." The Jew, added Wagner, in building on his stereotype, "rules, and will rule, so long as Money remains the power before which all our doings and our dealings lose their force." To Wagner, "Judaism is the evil conscience of our modern Civilisation."

Thus, from Wagner's perspective, it was natural to argue that German culture needed to be purged of Jewish influence. "But if emancipation from the yoke of Judaism appears to us the greatest of necessities," he wrote, "we must hold it weighty above all to prove our forces for this war of liberation."

With uncanny prescience, Wagner spoke of immolating Jews, according to a December 18, 1881, entry in the diary of Cosima Wagner, his second wife: "Richard says as a vehement joke that all the Jews ought to be burnt at a performance of 'Nathan the Wise.'"

These philosophies are ingrained in Wagner's life and music. Like Wiesel, I, too, can go a lifetime without hearing another note of Wagner's work, though I must concede I say so having already heard these scores and studied their breakthroughs.

More painful, to me, is the case of Frédéric Chopin, perhaps the greatest composer for the piano (at least until Maurice Ravel). Take away Chopin's ballades and nocturnes, sonatas and scherzos, preludes and waltzes, and the piano repertoire is left with a looming hole at its center. Even if I were to swear off listening to Chopin, his music still would play in my inner ear every day, as it always has. I cannot forget this music, and I cannot conceive of the piano without Chopin.

And yet his poisonous words injure.

"I did not expect that Pleyel would Jew me; but, if so, please give him this letter," wrote Chopin in a letter on March 13, 1839, in discussing music publishers. "If I have got to deal with Jews, let it at least be Orthodox ones. Probst may swindle me even worse, for he's a sparrow whose tail you can't salt. Schlesinger has always cheated me; but he has made a lot out of me, and won't want to refuse another profit; only be polite to him, because the Jew likes to pass for somebody."

And on March 17, 1839: "Good Lord, why must one have dealings with scoundrels! That Pleyel, who told me that Schlesinger was underpaying me, and now finds 500 fr. too much for a manuscript for all countries! Well, I prefer to do business with a real Jew. And Probst is a rascal to pay me 300 for the mazurkas! Why, the last mazurkas brought me 800 at the first jump: Probst 300, Schl. 400, Wess. 100. I would rather sell my manuscripts for nothing as in the old days, than have to bow and scrape to such fools. And I'd rather be humiliated by one Jew than by 3."

I must work hard to separate this bigotry from the ineffably poetic music Chopin penned, and I know I will never be able to resolve the dissonance between them. Wagner is easier to set aside, thanks to the often insufferable bombast of the music and the pervasiveness of the anti-Semitism. Chopin is more difficult, because of the exquisite transparency of the work and the less-heated quality of the hatred of Jews.

In both cases and others, however, the paradox of high art and hateful intentions cannot be reconciled.

The anti-Semitism that permeates the history of Western music stands as a reflection of hatreds widely held. Which led me to ask Wiesel, If geniuses such as Wagner and Chopin can nurture such enmities, what hope is there for the rest of humanity?

Wiesel answered my question with one of his own. "If Auschwitz didn't cure the world of anti-Semites, what will and what can?" he asked. Even today, "they say we control the press. And I said, '*Halevi*,'" he added, invoking a Yiddish term that roughly means "if only" or "let it be."

"I wish it were so," he added. "The anti-Semites say that you control the world. I said, 'OK, give us the world for one year. And I promise, when we give it back, it won't be worse. But give it to us!'

"Once I was in Prague at a conference, an international conference with fifty or sixty intellectuals from all over the world, famous names," continued Wiesel, who was astonished at the anti-Semitic observations some of these thinkers said to his face. He responded with equal directness.

"Hey, wait a second—you really believe that we Jews control the media, we control Wall Street, we control everything?" he told them. "You know what? Give the world to us for one generation. Not more. I promise you—we'll give it back to you, it won't be worse. But it isn't so!"

And yet there's a conundrum here. For even as Wiesel told me that he considers anti-Semitism the most ancient and enduring group hatred, he also contended that "no other people of antiquity survived antiquity the way we did."

How is this possible? How has such a timeless hatred failed to destroy its long-intended target?

To explain why Jewish culture and life have survived despite timeless efforts to eradicate it, Wiesel cited his first meeting with the Dalai Lama, who sought his counsel long ago.

"Teach us the art of the survival," Wiesel recalled the Dalai Lama saying to him. "After all, you, the Jews, left the homeland two thousand years ago, and you are here still. My people just left it, but I know it's going to be a long way in exile. So teach us the art of survival."

Wiesel told the Dalai Lama that Jews prevailed for various reasons, but "the first one really is that when other people left their homelands, they took money, they took jewels with them. But when we left ours, we took one little thing: a book. A small book. But that book produced thousands and thousands of other books. And it is our attachment to the book" that explains Jews' survival in the face of unrelenting genocide, said Wiesel.

By referencing "the book," Wiesel referred not only to religious texts but also, of course, to related cultural traditions and practices.

"It means learning—the passion for learning," he explained. "When we left Egypt, we had only the book, the little book. That little book is what? The Ten Commandments. At the beginning the Ten Commandments, then the Prophecies and so forth. All the Ten Commandments actually have almost nothing to do with God but with our human relations: 'Thou shalt not steal.'

"God said [in effect], 'I can take care of myself, don't worry about it. You can take care of my other children,'" added Wiesel, offering a colloquial interpretation.

"I think that little book, therefore, represented a passion of learning. That little book produced so many hundreds and hundreds and thousands and thousands of more books. And that is really what kept us when we had nothing. We didn't take jewels. We took that little book. And that little book accompanies us wherever we go, wherever we stay.

"And we study every single day. And we obey—we try to obey, at least. We can, if you are religious. The main thing is, without the book— we are called the People of the Book. Muhammad gave us the title— without the book, where would we be? Converted somewhere, so many other places. There were attempts."

But surely there is more to it than this. Aside from reverence for the word, I asked Wiesel, why did Jews survive millennia of anti-Semitism before the Holocaust and, astonishingly, the decades after?

He pondered the question and, of course, raised another.

"The easiest answer, but the truest answer: faith in something superior and eternal," he said. "For the religious Jew, suffering was not only he suffers—it's also God suffering.

"And what about God, who looks down and sees what some of his children are doing to his other children?" added Wiesel, clearly referring to the perpetrators of the Holocaust.

"That is the question," said Wiesel, "and only He could answer."

7

Where Did We Go Wrong?

We grapple with questions that Wiesel said only God could answer. Still, we struggle to divine how this could have happened.

I never asked my parents how they tried to understand, and so now I asked Wiesel.

He responded, as he often did, with a question.

"We speak about the mountain of knowledge . . . one story after the other after the other," Wiesel said. "And you say that all that produced Auschwitz? Where did we go wrong?"

In other words, Wiesel seemed to be saying, if five-thousand-plus years of human history led us to the Holocaust, we must step back and try to find where the wrong turn occurred. Where civilization—including even music—went astray.

More specifically, how a society that produced Bach and Beethoven and Goethe could have culminated in a culture of death. One would think that certain books, certain poems, certain symphonies, certain essays on philosophy and morality might make humanity invulnerable to evil, Wiesel said.

That "somebody who knows how to decipher a poem by Goethe and to describe the depth of the beauty of a painting by Rembrandt, they cannot do certain things," as Wiesel put it to me.

We try to believe this even as we know that the examples of Wagner, Chopin, and others argue pointedly to the contrary. Even as we understand that many SS leaders held PhDs; that many German generals belonged to old, distinguished, aristocratic families. These people were steeped in the philosophy of one of the most advanced civilizations on earth.

How could they?

"Yes, philosophy was there," Wiesel said, but "ethos was not. They did not study ethics. Therefore, I go around America and the world, really, lobbying in every university: you must include lessons on ethos, ethics, because without it, all the other things are almost meaningless.

"I think I read every single book that appeared on the subject [of the Holocaust], in at least five languages available to me. And I am still waiting for a psychological book on that saying, What happened to the psyche of the victimizer? What happened to the psyche" to allow him to do such things?

By ethos, Wiesel did not mean the dictionary definition: "the characteristic and distinguishing attitudes, habits, beliefs, etc. of an individual or a group." Instead he referred to something more tailored to the discussion at hand: the codes and laws and values by which individuals relate to one another.

For Jews who believe, ethos is "the most important thing," he said. The most crucial issues in the Bible, he added, are "not things between me and God but things between me and you. What you do to your fellow human being, always. And that is ethos."

Ethos, in other words, implies consideration of and respect for "the other," as Wiesel put it. More specifically, each of us has a moral obligation not only to each other but to "the other," who is outside our sphere of familiarity, he maintained.

"To defend those who need defense, to offer your presence to those who are lonely, console those who lost someone, comfort those who are sick," he said.

The architects of the Holocaust took the inverse position, afflicting "the other," which of course meant Jews but also gay people, political dissidents, Roma, Christian Science believers, and others. Yet it's pivotal to remember that the Jew stood at the center of this field of outsiders, the primary target, the raison d'être for the Holocaust.

A friend of mine who converted to Christian Science in her young adulthood often protested to me that those of her faith who were killed by Nazis for their beliefs were no different than those who were killed for being Jews. To be killed is to be killed, she said. To be persecuted is to be persecuted, she insisted. The two groups were the same; their fate was the same. They were equal.

I disagreed, but Wiesel's explanation expressed the difference between the two fates more succinctly than I ever was able to convey to my friend: Though not all victims were Jews, Wiesel said, all Jews were victims. There was no escape from this identity and, therefore, from this fate. A drop of Jewish blood was a death sentence, Hitler proved. And that judgment was declared even before a Jew was born. No Jew would be spared; an entire people would be obliterated.

Amid this genocide (a word coined by a Polish Jew, Raphael Lemkin, in the midst of the Holocaust), men who lived in a world of high art and rarefied thought—the province of Kant and Hegel, Mozart and Beethoven, Wagner and Chopin—overlooked the value of a singular creation: the human being.

Were the Nazis too cut off from society? I asked Wiesel.

"Not from society—from Jews," he said. "They learned that Jews are not human beings."

This is evident not only in Wagner's rantings but also in Nazi-era documents, particularly those dispatched to the Einsatzgruppe, the units that swept across Eastern Europe early in the war, machine-gunning Jews by the tens of thousands. These were the same German soldiers who drove through my mother's little village, Dubno, in what was then easternmost Poland, and executed nearly the entire Jewish population there, twelve thousand in all. The victims were deemed "vermin" and "bacillus," according to Nazi documents, which on this basis sought to justify their extermination.

No Jew would be spared, no mercy accorded children or the elderly. The very young were targeted because in killing a child, "they kill the past—not only the future, but also the past," said Wiesel. By this I believe he meant that any memory of the past would be extinguished by executing the young, who can carry memories forward.

"And that was a kind of total killing," said Wiesel.

Or "you can put it more brutally," he continued. "The children because of their future, and the old because of their past. It's not six million Jews. It's six million times that a Jew was assassinated, and each one with his own history and destiny and memory."

Another way of saying this is to conclude that the Nazis wished not only to kill individuals but also to wipe out identity. This was a "meta-historical" approach to murder, as Wiesel termed it, and it went well beyond body count.

"It encompassed every endeavor, every aspect, every facet, it encompassed the totality of the Jewish being," said Wiesel.

More specifically, Wiesel has argued, the targets of the Holocaust were us, the second generation.

"It was you that the enemy sought to destroy," Wiesel said in his keynote address at the First International Conference of Children of Holocaust Survivors in New York in 1984. "We were only the instruments. You were the enemy's obsession. In murdering living Jews, he wished to prevent you from being born. He knew how vulnerable we Jews are with regard to children. Our history begins with a Jewish child, Isaac, being threatened but then saved. It continues with Jewish children being massacred by Pharaoh, Nebuchadnezzar and Titus, Haman and Hitler—all our enemies saw our children as the primary target."

This may seem like an esoteric, rarefied way of looking at mass slaughter, but surely it's grounded in the core meaning of genocide. Moreover, it resonates in Jewish history, in that the killing of Jewish children, for instance, was hardly an innovation of Hitler's. It has been the modus operandi among anti-Semites going back to the story of Passover.

For this reason, the Holocaust must be considered a particularly Jewish event, "a Jewish tragedy," as Wiesel put it, "but with universal implications and applications." Yes, there are broad lessons to be learned from the Holocaust. But the universality of the Holocaust, said Wiesel, "lies in its identity. It was a Jewish identity."

This may not be the politically correct view of an event that targeted so many demonized groups. But the yellow Star of David that Jews were forced to wear—the same yellow Star of David my mother now believes has been sewn onto every scrap of her clothing—symbolizes the central meaning and purpose of the Holocaust. What did the Germans burn first as they invaded Eastern European villages? The synagogues. Where did the first executions begin in my mother's town and uncounted others? The Jewish cemetery.

What was Hitler obsessed with, even after losing Stalingrad and retreating on two fronts?

"That they have not killed enough Jews yet," said Wiesel.

And for all the killings of Jews in biblical times and thereafter, all the pogroms that decimated Jews in Russia and Eastern Europe through the centuries, the Holocaust was different in many regards, but especially one.

"For the first time in history conversion was not a solution, not even for the converts," said Wiesel. "There were, in the Warsaw ghetto, converts that had their own barracks, their own church. Even for the converts, there was no escape. What was the escape? Only into death."

This was the Final Solution, and no one was less prepared to understand it than its primary victims. Jews under these dire circumstances were "literally innocent, in the same sense as naive," Wiesel said to me. He meant that Jews—even after millennia of persecution—simply did not imagine that it was possible for human beings to do what the Nazis intended.

Moreover, during World War I, the Germans had saved Jews from the pogroms of the Russians. The Germans' plans in World War II, therefore, were not readily anticipated, known, or understood to most Jews when the Nazis arrived in their towns and shtetls—even as late as 1944, as they entered Sighet, Wiesel's village in Transylvania.

"Everybody knew, except we," said Wiesel, referencing his family and neighbors.

The same was true across Europe: Jews were unaware of what awaited them. Many Holocaust survivors I've interviewed over the years have said the same haunting phrase to me, over and over: "If only we knew." If only they knew that the trains were going to Auschwitz, they told me, they would have tried to escape the ghettos, even as they were being marched to the rail station. If only they knew what Auschwitz meant, they would have risked everything to run. If only.

But they didn't know, even though much of the rest of the world did.

When the German Wehrmacht arrived, "wherever it came," said Wiesel, there was relief at first. "So I come back to my own Maria," said Wiesel, referring to the Christian woman who worked as housekeeper for the Wiesel family in Sighet and begged them to flee with her when they still could. She wanted them to live out the war with her family in the hinterlands.

"Our maid was an illiterate Christian woman—she was a saint in my eyes," said Wiesel. "In the ghetto, she came to plead with my father.

"She said, 'Mr. Wiesel, don't go [on the trains]. Come, I have a hut in the mountains, and you'll stay with me. I will feed you.'

"We would have had the whole family survive, if only we would have known," Wiesel added.

"We listened to the radio in the ghetto. If Roosevelt had made a speech and Churchill a speech: 'Jews in Hungary, now it's your turn. We urge you: Don't go to the railway station. Don't go because there is someplace called Auschwitz. Don't go to the railway station.'

"Maybe not all of us would have listened," continued Wiesel. "But I can tell you a high percentage would have gone to the forest and wanted to save their lives. I found after the war that before 1942 the *New York Times* already had it, on page sixteen or something," said Wiesel, with a dark laugh, "a story about the liquidation of European Jewry. And we didn't know? Well, there was one who came back from such, but we thought he was crazy."

This, of course, was Moishe the Beadle, who, in the pages of Wiesel's *Night*, told the disbelieving Jews of Sighet of the massacre he somehow had survived. But no one would believe him or could believe him.

"We thought he was crazy. But Roosevelt was our God," said Wiesel. "I didn't hear his name until I came to New York. But Roosevelt—he was the father figure of the Jewish people.

"If he had said, 'My friends, Jews in Hungary, now it's your turn, we know what they are planning. You don't, but we know. Don't go! The first step is the most important one. Go and hide. Don't go to the railway station.' Not all, but some, if not most, would [have] run away."

In repeating this imagined scenario to me over and over again, Wiesel seemed to be wishing it into reality, trying to make it so through repetition, yearning to turn back the clock to what might have been, to try to unravel past tragedies. By 1944, of course, the war was nearly over, and still no one told the Jews of Eastern Europe what awaited them.

Yet even if they had, Wiesel's retrospective hopes may have been too optimistic. Many Jews might have run away, but surely many, if not most, would have been killed in the attempt. Even so, there's added pain in realizing that the victims had not even a warning.

"And we should have known because we were affected by it, more than the others," Wiesel said to me. "Then the question is, And what if we had known? We, after all, intelligent people, went to school, loved literature, wrote letters, all of that, and all of a sudden somebody comes and tells you: 'Hey, do you know what people are capable of doing? Those people you went to school with and so forth—they were murderers?'

"Why go believe that? Why should we? It would be abnormal to believe that."

Wiesel wrote searingly about this disbelief in *Night*, when Moishe the Beadle told of how Jews had been forced to dig trenches—their own crude mass graves—before being shot and tumbling into them, one by one, family by family, village by village. This is exactly what happened in my mother's little Dubno, the story she never told me.

"But people not only refused to believe his tales, they refused to listen," wrote Wiesel in *Night*. "Some even insinuated that he only wanted their pity, that he was imagining things. Others flatly said that he had gone mad."

Of course, he had gone mad—precisely because these horrendous killings had happened and he had very nearly succumbed to them. When Moishe the Beadle described these murders, the young Wiesel had only one reaction, he told me: he pointed to his head, as if to say anyone who said such things must be crazy.

Therein lies another level of meaning behind this template for genocide. Was it conceived on such a grandiose scale precisely because no one would believe that it would be possible?

"Was it planned and programmed by an enemy that thought, 'They won't believe, they won't believe'?" asked Wiesel.

In other words, were the atrocities conceived to be of such an incalculable magnitude so that they could not be comprehended or accepted? That the scope of this killing would be too staggering to be absorbed by anyone afterward, not even from the testimony of those who miraculously might survive?

Certainly survivors often have said to me that "there are no words" to describe what happened. The killings exceeded the reach of language and, also tragically, the capability of the human psyche to cope with them.

Thus my mother struggled for decades to hide her autobiography from me and my sister and from herself, only to have it come roaring back when she was old and most vulnerable. The human psyche cannot manage calamity of this scope and degree, as my mother's mental breakdown attests. The scale of these events boggles and shatters the mind. The losses engendered grief that was "unresolved and unresolvable," in the writings of Dr. Joel Sadavoy.

"Nothing is for this," said Wiesel. "Nothing is for this scale. Writing is not for this scale. It never happened before in history. Look, we Jews knew about pogroms.

"But here is a cultured people—the Germans—that have the best of its people, the best minds, come up with creating an Auschwitz? And they worked on it. They all worked on it. They really created a new industry, a new capital of crime. It created Auschwitz to the last detail: How to bring the victims to Birkenau and the trains. Everything was worked out. They had their own psychologists, their own sociologists, their own philosophers, their own theologians, their own chemists.

"Everything was worked out. The best. And they sat down in their laboratories to work on that? It's what you said—mind boggling," added Wiesel. "It deranged the mind. It means, a normal mind cannot conceive of that possibility."

And so when Moishe the Beadle came to Sighet to tell of the massacre, "we didn't believe him, I didn't believe him," said Wiesel again, apparently so frustrated by his past disbelief that he kept returning to it. "Come on. Really. You really tell me that people are doing mass killing? No, really. In the twentieth century?"

Even now—after all we know, after all the books and all the research—we cannot adequately frame the story of the Holocaust. The breadth of the event expands the more we study and the more we learn. Recent research at the United States Holocaust Memorial Museum in Washington, DC, has begun to document the inexorably expanding scope of the Holocaust. When the studies began in 2000, researchers had expected to find 7,000 Nazi ghettos and camps across Europe. So far, they have documented 42,500 and counting.

The toll continues to rise. And Wiesel told me he wonders what God does with this knowledge.

8

The Scene of the Crimes

In 2003 and 2004, I traveled to Dubno, where my mother was born and from where she fled as a child, to search for answers.

Years before that, Wiesel had made a similar journey, to the Polish town of Oświęcim, or Auschwitz in English, also pursuing elusive truths.

"I was there, and I tried to understand the inhabitants of Auschwitz the town," he told me. "How did they live? It was seven kilometers from the camp. What is seven kilometers? Four miles. You can walk. What did they think, the inhabitants of this town?"

In effect, Wiesel was trying to answer one of his most pressing and enduring questions: How did ordinary people commit extraordinary crimes or, at least, allow them to happen? What happened to seemingly decent, everyday people to enable them to countenance unspeakable acts? How did they do it? Why did they do it? And how did it change them?

While Wiesel was in Oświęcim, he told me, he noticed two men on the street speaking English to one another.

"I listened and came to them, I introduced myself," he told me. "One of them was a priest, and his brother who was a local.

"And I said, 'Who are you?'

"He said, 'This is my brother, he lives in America, and he came to visit me.'"

Wiesel asked the priest's brother, a resident of Oświęcim, exactly where he lived.

"He showed me his house," continued Wiesel.

"I said, 'Actually I came to visit—where was Birkenau?'

"And he said, 'There—right there,'" continued Wiesel, with a bitter laugh. The horrors in this sprawling complex of camps and subcamps, in other words, were not so far from this man's front door.

"Wait a second—show me," Wiesel said to him, pressing the point.

"There!" said the man, pointing to the obvious, as they walked in that direction.

"So I said, 'Did you know?'"

This was a portentous question, for to say that, yes, the man knew a death camp was so near would be to acknowledge a kind of passive complicity, at least. But to say no would be to deny the obvious truth.

"He said, 'Of course, how could you not know? We lived here,'" Wiesel recalled.

Now Wiesel began to dig more deeply.

"Where was the camp?" Wiesel asked, inquiring simply about facts, not morality. At least not yet.

"He said, 'It was there,'" pointing into the distance.

Indeed, "there was the camp, the iron gate," recalled Wiesel.

Then Wiesel cut to the heart of the matter. "Did you know?" he asked the man, referring to what went on behind the gate.

"Of course we knew," the local man acknowledged, without pause or hesitation.

Wiesel pushed further, into the dark secrets of this story. "How did you know?" Wiesel asked the man.

"He said, 'Because I heard the gong every morning, how they got up. And we saw them from the window. We saw them inside the gate.'"

The "them," of course, being Wiesel and the others.

"I said to him, 'Describe to me your morning. At what time did you get up?'" said Wiesel, recounting his methodical, prosecutorial inquiry. "'And what did you see at the gate?'"

Wiesel wanted details, the nuts and bolts of everyday life as it was lived outside the hellish place. Perhaps he hoped to learn how ordinary men and women would weave such horrors into their daily life cycles yet turn away.

"He said, 'I got up usually at six o'clock. They were already standing in line,'" Wiesel said, quoting the gentleman.

The man did not know that Wiesel was among those standing and waiting for hours to be counted and, eventually, barely fed.

"I remember, they were standing in line for bread," the man said.

As Wiesel and his father waited for sustenance, this man had seen the events from afar. The disconnect between such suffering and such nonchalant observation of it must have been difficult for Wiesel to hear. He told me that he continued his questioning.

"I said, 'Did you sleep well at night?'" Wiesel asked. He laughed bitterly as he said this, clearly in recognition of the moral reckoning at the heart of the question.

"In the beginning no, but afterward yes," the man said.

The response sounded sadly believable: the man was disturbed at first but then came to accommodate or accept the circumstances, or rationalize them. A kind of banal indifference at best, a tragic disregard at worst.

"Naturally," said Wiesel to me, noting the perverse avoidance of so many to such suffering.

I told Wiesel it still seemed incomprehensible to me that a continent could accept the kind of inhumanity the man in Oświęcim had grown so inured to. And here Wiesel offered his analysis of the crux of the matter: how it happened.

"It was not a maniac alone who gathered around another one hundred or one thousand or ten thousand maniacs," said Wiesel, referring to Hitler and his millions of enthusiastic followers. "It was part of the system, part of the philosophy, part of the ideology, everything, part of their way of living was to kill Jews. It was their religion. It was their obsession. It was their goal in life. For the killers, the goal in life was to kill ten thousand Jews a day.

"I'm sure if you would ask a child of the SS, 'When you grow up, what do you want to do?'" the answer would be predictable, said Wiesel. "'Like my father: kill ten thousand Jews a day.'"

The aftereffects of this mind-set resonate today, in my mother's daytime nightmare, in the toll of those lost, in the children who never were born. Even as the war ground on to its inevitable finish, even when the Germans clearly were vanquished, the killing had to continue, the people of Wiesel's Sighet had to be rounded up and shipped to Auschwitz.

"In 1944, they lost the war already," said Wiesel, as if to protest. And yet "with us it began then. The first ghetto was in March. The first deportation was in May 1944, two weeks before D-day. They had lost the war. Nevertheless, it became their priority.

"They needed every train for their military troops. Nevertheless, the priority was to deport the Jews. When you read all the documents today, you don't understand it. It doesn't seem logical. It doesn't seem profitable. They had other things on their mind. They were losing the war. Nevertheless, their priority was to kill Jews."

If Wiesel's recollection of his trip to Auschwitz-Birkenau prompted a sobering analysis from him, it also reminded me of the one and only time my parents returned to the scene of the crimes. Shortly after my father retired from the bakery and not long before his illness struck, he and my mother and several relatives decided to return to Poland for the first (and last) time since the war, four decades later.

My parents packed for weeks for this trip, loading up multiple suitcases in their tiny Skokie living room as if preparing not for a vacation trip but for another exodus. They invited me to join them, but at that point in my life, I still was avoiding any contact with this overwhelming story. I declined. Unfortunately.

Years later, I studied pictures of the visit, my father looking pale at his return to his past life and his visit to Auschwitz, where he presumed his parents and most of his siblings had been killed. At my father's funeral, a friend of his read a eulogy recounting the events of the return to Europe.

"The family had gone back to Poland and to the town of his birth and early life," he said. "Remember that the occupation of the Nazis had indelibly changed all the memories of joy into macabre scenes of deprivation, torture, and unspeakable horror.

"As the family walked through the town, they came upon the old family home, now lived in by some elderly lady, and when they came up to the house, the lady ran out and started to run away—probably to hide. It was Robert who went after her and called out to her not to run, for he understood the circumstances of her living there, and he was not going to make trouble but only wanted to look again at his childhood home . . . such kindness in the ashes of such hell."

I don't know exactly what my father thought of his homecoming to Sosnowiec and his trip to Auschwitz—the unmarked graveyard of his parents and most of his siblings—what nightmares it stirred in him. We never discussed it. I never felt right asking him, and I surely feared hearing the tale. But I imagine his reaction was not unlike Wiesel's, both a sorrowful recognition and an enduring shock that it could have happened in the first place. A web of belief and disbelief.

After my parents came back to Skokie from their pilgrimage to the past, I learned that my mother had declined to visit her hometown of Dubno. At the time, I didn't understand why. Her mental breakdown years later helped explain it: going would have been disastrous for her, and she knew it.

I've spent most of my life like her, afraid to get too close to this subject. I told Wiesel that I find it almost impossible to watch movies about the Nazis or the Holocaust or to read documents on these events, except in journalistic projects, at which point I go into work mode and mute personal feelings, or try to.

"I like to read all of that," countered Wiesel. "Not that I like it, to enjoy it. But I want to know more. There isn't a book that comes out on that subject that I don't read, if the language is appropriate, that I know.

"Each time I hope I will find an answer. The answer is not how. How, I know. Because they invested all their knowledge—scientific and political and economic—they invested everything they had, really, to kill Jews. Strange how they think about it.

"But why? Why? Why did it happen? And that question remains to me an open question. Why did Auschwitz happen? Why? I don't have the answer to that.

"How, I know. They used their own psychologists and their psychiatrists and their scientists, how to fool the Jews, how to cheat them, how to treat them.

"It was science. For them it was science to kill Jews. OK, we know. The order was given, the decision was made. Naturally they were scientific and practical, pragmatic. They knew what to do. Unfortunately they knew. Unfortunately from their viewpoint they did well.

"But why? Why? I don't know. And that question is troubling me and plaguing me to this day and this night. I don't know. Why? Why? Why did it happen?"

Of course, as Wiesel himself has indicated, these questions cannot be suitably answered by us. Nevertheless, we struggle with them.

"Lately I ask myself the question from a religious viewpoint," he said. "To those who believe in God, there is reward and punishment—the basis of morality and religious morality as well. What sins could the Jewish people have committed until the war that justified the murder of six million Jews?"

I quoted to Wiesel the oft-cited claim that Jews killed Christ, never a really compelling answer for the "why" of the Holocaust.

"No, no, look," said Wiesel. "That played for the pogroms, but not for the Germans. In Hitler's and Goebbels's documents, you don't have Christ mentioned. They had other things but not Christ."

So I cited the Nazi documents labeling Jews as "vermin" and "bacillus" and other dehumanizing terms.

"Subhumans, subhumans," Wiesel concurred. "Sure. But nevertheless we control the world, we subhumans control the world, and therefore we control Roosevelt, we control Churchill, and we control everybody. We are there, we give commands—we give orders to the armies. We Jews in the ghettos were giving orders to the armies. It's absurd.

"OK, this is the how. But why? I don't know. From any viewpoint, I don't understand the why. Why Auschwitz? I don't know."

We are left in an untenable but inescapable position. As a character in Wiesel's novel *Gates of the Forest* notes: If so many millions died for no reason, it's an insult. And if they died for a reason, it's even more an insult.

We feel this today and forevermore. Another paradox that cannot be resolved.

9

How Did Our Parents Stay Sane?

After the war, after all they endured, after all they lost, the survivors suffered another blow: the newfound knowledge that the rest of the world knew much of what was happening.

The European Jews' agonies were known in Washington and beyond as early as 1942, a fact most recently underscored in "Americans and the Holocaust," an exhibition at the United States Holocaust Memorial Museum that also shows the roots of indifference. It includes a 1935 quote from Roosevelt projected on a wall: "The German authorities are treating the Jews shamefully and the Jews in this country are greatly excited. But this is also not a governmental affair." In a 1938 movie newsreel shown in theaters nationwide, "Inside Nazi Germany," the narrator notes that the German regime is "pitilessly" persecuting Jews. This campaign made scant impact on America and the rest of the world during the killing.

And after.

This is what the survivors learned following their ordeals and losses, adding to their psychic burden.

Such neglect haunts Wiesel "to this day," he said to me. "In the beginning, the world didn't even know the extent of Hitler's barbaric technology," he added, as if struggling to find some explanation for official apathy in the early years of the war.

"Believe me, I don't know" why so many did so little, added Wiesel. "Because when I came to America in 1956, and I went to the sources—archives and so forth—I came to realize that people knew. We thought that people didn't know. We in Auschwitz, we said to each other, 'Ach, if only the world knew.'

"And afterward I learned: 'Oh, the world knew.' That's why my book *Night* actually originally was called *And the World Was Silent*. In Yiddish, *Un di Velt Hot Geshvign*.

"They knew. How is it possible, really, that *we* didn't know? But the fact is we didn't. When we came to Auschwitz, and I remember my father and all of us, from the train, we saw Auschwitz—it evoked nothing. Nineteen forty-four! A few days before D-day, May 1944. Washington knew. The Vatican knew. Switzerland knew. Stockholm knew. Everybody knew. Except we."

After the war, the survivors quickly came to see their insignificance in the grand scheme of things and observe the marginalization of their stories, their losses, their heroism. Almost every survivor I've interviewed has told me that when they came to America, people told them to "forget about it," "put it behind you," "you're in America now," "start over."

The Polish Catholic Auschwitz survivor Zofia Posmysz—whose radio play *Passenger in Cabin 45* was adapted by composer Mieczyslaw Weinberg and librettist Alexander Medvedev into the devastating Holocaust opera *The Passenger*—remembered receiving precisely this advice from someone quite close to her.

"My mother asked me to take her [to Auschwitz] because she wanted to know how I lived—pay attention to the word—*lived*," Posmysz told me of her first return to the death camp, in June 1945. She had been enslaved there from 1942 to 1945 for pursuing classroom studies that had been banned by the Nazis and for having associated with fellow students who carried anti-Nazi leaflets.

Posmysz, who has lived in Poland ever since, did not wish to return to Auschwitz immediately after the war, "but I couldn't say no to my mother, and we went together," she continued. "There was no museum at the time. It was just an open area, which you could enter. So I went to the first barracks, where I was when I was ill with typhus, and I showed her the bed on which I was lying. And she said, 'Poor thing. These are not beds, these are drawers.'

"And she never asked anything again and didn't want to continue that visit. And when we came back home, she started to cry and said, 'You will never go there again. You have to forget it.'"

Wiesel experienced the same thing, as did uncounted others he knew. Survivors, he said, repeatedly were told, "Don't speak about it, we know," he remembered. "Don't talk about it. Look, now live here in America, in a free country, where happiness is part of the Constitution. Really. Turn the page. Forget."

Forgetting would be impossible, but, in any event, few listeners really wanted to hear the gruesome stories. Even psychiatrists often were unwilling to sit still for these narratives, research has shown. Instead, psychiatrists frequently steered survivors away from telling the tale, weaving what Dr. Milton E. Jucovy—a psychiatrist who documented this phenomenon—called a "curtain of silence." "It seemed necessary for both survivors and the external world to forget," wrote Jucovy, who was only half right, because the survivors never were going to forget.

Yet the survivors got the message. "Denial and repression reigned during this period of silence," wrote Jucovy. So Wiesel's original title for what became *Night* was prescient, for the world was silent not only during the Holocaust but after as well, adding to the survivors' pain.

But why was it this way? Why such disinterest?

"You know why," Wiesel said to me. "It was too sad. They didn't want to publish my book *Night* because it was too morbid, they said." Indeed, multiple publishers rejected the manuscript, even as Nobel laureate François Mauriac championed it. And when *Night* finally was published, it sold poorly for a generation.

"In the beginning, people didn't want to hear the story, it's true," said Wiesel. "Didn't want to hear. The very first books that came out were usually diaries. And people didn't want to hear. I understood. How can I judge someone who doesn't want to hear that kind of horror? I understand it. So few documents, autobiographies, were published immediately after. People didn't want to hear, so publishers didn't want to publish. But then, slowly, the story developed."

There were other reasons the world chose not to listen. Not surprisingly, we return to anti-Semitism. The identity of the victims was central here.

"They said, 'Well, it's only Jews,'" Wiesel told me. "Look at the *New York Times*. The *New York Times*! As a former journalist, after all, that's the bible of our profession, right? When you check in the archives, how it cut coverage, it's embarrassing. It's scandalous.

"When everybody knew already, when it was official. Even the first story, the official story from the State Department about mass killings— it was hidden somewhere inside the paper. So if the *New York Times* and the press hid it, why should people know?"

Indeed, as Wiesel said, the *New York Times*—then and now the most influential newspaper in America—soft-pedaled the news, as Laurel Leff documented in her definitive study, *Buried by the Times: The Holocaust and America's Most Important Newspaper*. Rabbi Stephen S. Wise, head of the New York–based World Jewish Congress in the early 1940s, had learned in August 1942 of the Nazis' machinery to deport Jews, Leff wrote. Under Secretary of State Sumner Welles asked Wise to hold off making an announcement until the information could be confirmed.

Wise and the World Jewish Congress had to wait until November 24, 1942, for State Department confirmation. By then, millions of Jews had been killed, including most of the twelve thousand in my mother's village of Dubno. Rabbi Wise "learned through sources confirmed by the State Department that about half the estimated 4,000,000 Jews in Nazi-occupied Europe had been slain in an 'extermination campaign,'" according to an AP story that ran in the *New York Times* on November 25, 1942. On page 10.

This was typical of coverage in the *Times* and in newspapers across the country. Between September 1939 and May 1945, Leff showed, the *Times* ran 1,186 stories about the fate of European Jews. The news of the unfolding Holocaust "made the *Times* front page just 26 times, and only in six of those stories were Jews identified on the front as the primary victims," wrote Leff. And "only two lead editorials on Jews throughout the war" appeared in the *Times*, Leff reported. This despite the fact that by December 1942, the United States, Britain, and the Allies had announced that they knew of the Nazis' systematic genocide against Jews.

Jewish newspapers, Wiesel acknowledged, did cover the mass killings of Jews during the war. But the monumental scope of the events and their place in the hierarchy of news often eluded even Jewish editors and writers. Wiesel remembered an incident in his own experience that eerily brought this point home.

"I read a dissertation years ago, when I came to America, written by an Israeli officer, about how the Jewish press treated what was happening," recalled Wiesel. "And it read like this: There were four Yiddish dailies, and they had on the front page: 'Another 100,000 killed' or 'a million killed.' Page two: 'Come and enjoy your summer vacation in the Catskills.'

"You know, he had to be hospitalized. He lost his mind, the officer who wrote this dissertation. Couldn't take it."

Wiesel himself had said many times to me that the scale of this genocide could not be absorbed by the human psyche, so we shouldn't be so surprised that daily journalism would downplay or try to diminish the impact of this bleak news. How much front-page coverage of mass killings and concentration camps would readers be willing to face before canceling their subscriptions?

Still, the breadth of journalistic indifference in relation to the scale of the killing seems incomprehensible in retrospect. Why would it be this way?

"You are the journalist, you tell me," said Wiesel. "They were not concerned. They didn't feel it was a story. Jews are suffering. What else is new? Jews are being persecuted again. What else is new? They didn't grasp the scope of it. Not only political, but the military, or social, the philosophical."

So it took generations for these stories to enter the cultural mainstream. Not until the ABC-TV network broadcast the flawed but nonetheless groundbreaking four-part miniseries *Holocaust* in 1978 would the subject enter American living rooms en masse. And then only in a sanitized, homogenized, diluted, distorted, and error-ridden form.

As Wiesel wrote in a *New York Times* essay on April 16, 1978, "Untrue, offensive, cheap: as a TV production, the film is an insult to those who perished and to those who survived." And yet until that week, culminating with the April 19 anniversary of the Warsaw ghetto uprising, the survivors did not exist in popular consciousness—not even in cheap and offensive form.

So Wiesel and my parents and the others learned early on the low value placed upon their losses and their suffering, at least by the rest of the world. Yes, there was news coverage. "Here and there, here and there," said Wiesel. "Almost against their will. Can you imagine, really, if I had been then a journalist, what I would have done?"

I can indeed imagine what Wiesel would have done if he had been in America during the war instead of in Auschwitz and Buchenwald. I can imagine because of what he did afterward. He clearly would have raised a cry of protest. He would have written articles and books and given lectures and buttonholed world leaders, just as he always did. But could even he have overcome a willful silence? We will never know, but we can guess.

Understanding that the world was uninterested in their war-era autobiographies, the survivors learned to speak of their tragedies mostly among themselves, focusing on struggling to survive again. They scattered across the globe, taught themselves new languages, found ways to earn a living, created new lives, built families. But they had been injured psychologically during the war and after, especially children like my mother.

As psychology professor Sarah Moskovitz observed in her landmark book, *Love Despite Hate: Child Survivors of the Holocaust and Their Adult Lives* (1983), "The loss of parents in early life means loss of the very nucleus of one's own identity." She noted "the continuing burden of loss the survivors feel for parents whom they have never known, a hunger for some link with the past through family connections destroyed or distorted, for traces of themselves buried in childhoods they dare not remember."

The survivors lost not only their family members, in other words, but also their ties to their own pasts, the essences of who they were. Moreover, many suffered symptoms of what eventually would be recognized as the post-traumatic stress disorder that has undone my mother. In 1964, psychiatrist William Niederland coined the term *survivor syndrome* to describe those marked for death who somehow managed to live but suffered afterward. They often experienced "increased arousal," "confusion between the present and the period of persecution (acting or feeling as if the traumatic event were recurring)," "psychotic and psychotic-like symptoms (illusions and hallucinations)," and "inability to verbalize the nature of the events," in the words of Dr. Joel Sadavoy in a journal of psychiatry. In effect, he summed up my mother's situation.

Sadavoy reported that an analysis of two hundred Holocaust survivors showed that 85 percent demonstrated survivor syndrome twenty to thirty years after the war. A 1969 study looked at 130 patients "who were believed to show no after-effects of the concentration camp experience," Sadavoy wrote, but researcher Dr. Paul Matussek "observed that, on closer inquiry, he did not see a single person without pathology."

How the survivors could continue to press forward amid massive losses, and how they maintained their sanity along the way, remains a mystery to me. Consider Polish survivor Posmysz's recollections of just one scene she witnessed in Auschwitz.

"Nineteen forty-four was the most horrible of all in that respect," she said to me. "It was the period where they were mass murdering Hungarian Jews, so the crematories were burning day and night."

One night, with dawn not far off, Posmysz was startled awake by an unfamiliar, eerie form of vocalizing. She went outside of her barracks to see what it was and witnessed "bodies on the grass," she said. "I didn't know if they were asleep or dead. They were lying there. And in the middle there was a man standing, and he was singing and raising his hands up. I didn't know what that was. And then I felt someone's hand on my shoulder."

Posmysz presumed she was being summoned by an Auschwitz over-seer, but when she turned around, she saw a Jewish prisoner who asked Posmysz if she knew what the man was singing.

"I said, 'It must be a prayer,'" remembered Posmysz.

"And she said, 'Yes, it's the Kaddish,'" the Hebraic prayer for the dead.

After sunrise, "there was nobody there, and there was smoke over the chimney of the crematory," added Posmysz. "So how can you live with that kind of image in your brain?"

How indeed? How did the survivors stay sane? How did Wiesel?

"I wasn't so sure I would," he said to me.

He pointed out that as part of his philosophy studies in Paris after the war he was required to take psychology courses, which entailed repeated visits to a mental hospital.

"I was afraid of that, and I was taken by that: insanity," he said. "That's why in every novel of mine there is always a madman. Look, to tell you that I know the answer, I don't. Logically, normally, I should have given in to despair or insanity or something, anyway, or total disbelief."

But Wiesel and so many others did not succumb to their demons, though my parents clearly struggled mightily against them. Alcohol helped my father try to sleep while my mother kept a vigil at the living room window. They were haunted.

Was there no psychiatric help?

"We tried after the war—psychiatrists and psychologists and psychotherapy—this is beyond that," said Wiesel. "I addressed conferences of psychotherapists and psychologists and psychiatrists—what do they know? Come on. The best and most experienced psychologists in the world know nothing compared to what a fifteen-year-old knows—knew—when he left from Auschwitz."

I'd always assumed psychiatrists knew a great deal because of their long years of schooling. But how could any amount of study prepare someone to comprehend the multiple, chronic traumas experienced by Holocaust survivors or prepare anyone for treating them? In this scenario, as Wiesel suggested, the patients had to have known much more than the doctors ever would. And words would not suffice for the survivors to tell their psychiatrists what had happened.

"When we came to France, I was young, sixteen, fifteen and a half, and we had, of course, educators," said Wiesel. "And they confessed to me later on. They were mainly beautiful young women who worked for the OSE, the organization that took care of the children. And they told me later they didn't even know what to do. They felt so helpless.

"And rightly so. Because we looked at them: What do they know about life? They want to be our teachers? We can become the teachers. We could ask them, What do you know about man? What do you know about mankind? What do you know about anything? You know nothing.

"And they felt it. Yet they had to educate us. When we left the camp and we came to France, we were in the children's home. They didn't know what to do because we knew so much more than our teachers about life and about everything. And they felt so helpless. They admitted it to me afterward. 'We knew that you were older than us,' they said. And yet they were ten years or twenty years older than us."

As Wiesel spoke these words, I remembered my father often saying that because of his experiences, he was different than the rest of us. "I have lived 120 years, I have lived two and three lives," he would say, baffling me by these comments when I was young. Yet his point was essentially the same as Wiesel's: After all my father had seen, he knew more than most of us ever could. He had lived more than one life. Who could tell him anything, really? And who could help him, or my mother, at least psychiatrically speaking?

Dr. Henry Krystal, a psychiatrist who broke new ground in understanding PTSD and a Holocaust survivor himself, came to the same conclusion. "I have to admit," he once wrote, "that my attempts to engage aging survivors of the Holocaust in psychoanalytic psychotherapy have been for the most part unsuccessful."

The survivors were on their own, having witnessed events they could not put into words and for which there was no willing audience, except other survivors. Nor were there cures for memories burned into their psyches. Even if my parents had sought psychiatric help, even if they had been able to trust a doctor enough to speak of their sacred losses, even if they had found the words, I doubt it would have made much of a difference. The memories would not go away.

"Why should they? Why should they?" said Wiesel, who long championed the value of memory, even at its most painful.

Yet my mother's memories have unraveled her life, leaving her unable to function in the world.

"It's normal, it's normal," said Wiesel. "In truth, those of us who do function are the exceptions."

As I asked Wiesel more about how the survivors managed to stay sane in the aftermath of insanity, he dramatically reframed the subject. The question wasn't simply how they stayed sane after the Holocaust, he said. "How did they stay sane during?" he asked. "During! Not to lose one's sanity inside. There is a miracle as great as the other one. The fact is that when two times two was not four but one hundred thousand," he added, referring metaphorically to the insanity of the times and, presumably, to the perversity of the Nazis' calculus of death. All the rules and norms of society, all the ethos of Jewish life had been cast aside, replaced by a macabre but hyperefficient German system of destroying Jews.

"And yet, and yet, we had to live, day after day, after day, after day, never knowing whether we will wake up in the morning," said Wiesel. "Never knowing whether my father, who is sleeping next to me, will get up. That means to live a normal life under these circumstances.

"How did we do it? I don't know. Maybe because we didn't have time to think. Maybe if I had to think that each time—to be afraid that my father next to me will not really survive in the camp—how could one live like that?"

In effect, Wiesel seemed to be saying, the survivors had to invent a new way of thinking about the reality around them in the midst of the Holocaust. I can't say I understand how they did that, how they recalibrated a way of perceiving life in which death was pervasive, in which each day could be the last, in which the laws of God on which they had been raised no longer applied.

The survivors were "living next to death or inside death," as Wiesel put it to me. And of course each survivor must have come to his or her own way of coping, or trying to. They had to attempt to find a kind of normalcy amid chaos and nihilism. Whether in death camps, like Wiesel and my father, or on the run, like my mother, the survivors somehow must have established a kind of mental order amid mayhem.

"Absolutely," said Wiesel. "But that is what can be said always about war, which is the most abnormal of all events. Simply, how is it possible to go on living in the most abnormal of events, when it's normal to kill, it's normal to be killed? How can one? And nevertheless we did. We had to."

The way the survivors reshaped their thinking perhaps helped enable them to survive. But that new framework for living and dying stayed with them after the war and imbued the way they behaved ever after—at least in the case of my parents. Their ways of thinking and reacting during their duress survived long after the war. Their psychic injuries, in other words, persisted. Most of the survivors lost parents and siblings at a very young age: 77 percent of child survivors lost both parents, according to one study.

"Which means the wound remains open," said Wiesel.

But, as usual, Wiesel also found the hopeful half of the equation. For he pointed out that despite all this, the survivors' ability to rebuild after the war—internal and external scars notwithstanding—attested to their resilience.

"It simply tells us that we are stronger than we think," he said. And then he quoted a French poet, who said, "Actually I am so weak that any pebble can kill me," recalled Wiesel. "But as long as I breathe—as long as I breathe!—I am immortal."

By that measure, the survivors were more immortal than most, having prevailed over the worst that humanity had to offer. They devoured new languages "as self-defense, self-preservation," said Wiesel. And they struggled to heal and rebuild.

My father spent a year after the war recuperating in a German hospital in Wiesbaden, he told me. My mother had one wish above all, her aunt Irene said to me: to flee Eastern Europe and come to America. Even the mysteries and challenges of a new country in which she didn't know the language were preferable to what she had seen and lived in Poland. It was not an easy transition.

My mother sometimes spoke of struggling to find her way to the job a social service agency had found for her in a Chicago factory. She often transferred to the wrong bus or missed her stop because she didn't understand the English words swirling around her. She told me of subsisting in one room in a boardinghouse in America, of being in debt from the outset, of waking up before sunrise every morning to put salve on acne-scarred skin, and of other travails she suffered after the war until she met and married my father, who rescued her from them.

"There were days and weeks I was hungry," said Wiesel, echoing my mother's postwar story. "I didn't make much of it. I was used to that. Hunger didn't bother me that much. I was hungry a lot of times. In Paris, many, many days of hunger."

Wiesel and my parents and other survivors overcame these hardships, but to him, an equal triumph was how they answered barbarity with civility. How they refused to allow the terrors to which they had been subjected to reduce them to responding in kind, to allow insanity to inspire more insanity. Instead, the vast majority of survivors renounced revenge, observed Wiesel.

"In the early years after the liberation, there were some survivors who believed in vengeance," he said. "Not many, but there were some.

"They said to us, 'We do to them.' We realized that's not the answer, to make other people suffer because we suffered. It's too simplistic. What is morality? It is the ability and the duty to say no," added Wiesel, picking up on a theme he often returned to. "Just that: no."

Revenge, added Wiesel, "is not the Jewish way." And, anyway, "if you start avenging, where do you start and where do you end? Do you start with the Hungarian fascists, the first to put together the Sighet ghetto and so forth? Or the Germans or the SS? Where do you start? How do you do that? We didn't have any experience in our history. We didn't know all that."

The survivors, Wiesel believed, "dealt very well" with the aftermath of their experiences, in an ethical sense. Despite psychological damage, they conducted themselves in humane ways, especially in light of their recent histories.

"Any psychiatrist will tell you—and I studied psychiatry—normally we should have chosen distress and despair," said Wiesel. "We didn't. We could have chosen crime, saying, 'We were dispossessed, whatever we had was taken away.' We could have said, 'Now it's your turn. And we need money. You didn't want to give it? We will take it.'

"I don't think that if you go into the archives you will find criminality among the survivors. Why not? The world was in turmoil, and they could have actually said, 'I don't believe in you anyway.' Why should they? No.

"There was something noble in their quest, to show that we remain human, we remain civilized, whatever the word means. Religious if we were, or antireligious if you became, although there was less of that, surprisingly. But simply human."

And yet the toll of their experiences weighed on them, in many ways, ever after.

10

Listening to Silence

I am surprised not that the survivors learned to be silent about their stories following the war but that they stayed silent for so long. Wiesel, for instance, fulfilled his promise to himself not to write about his experience for a full ten years.

He waited because "I was worried," he said. "I was worried that I will not find the right words. I was worried of using the wrong words, even worse. I still am not sure whether I found the words. I am not sure. But at least I said, 'I will wait ten years.'

"You know, ten in Jewish ritual is a special number. Ten years. So I waited. I kept my word."

He was not the only one. Yes, as Wiesel had indicated, some Holocaust memoirs were published immediately after the war, such as Primo Levi's *If This Is a Man* (1947, later published in the United States as *Survival in Auschwitz*) and Wladyslaw Szpilman's *Death of a City* (1946, later published in the United States as *The Pianist*, which survivor Roman Polanski made into a feature film in 2002).

But this was a trickle compared to the outpouring that would emerge decades later. In light of the ubiquity of this subject today, with newspapers carrying Holocaust-related stories almost every day on looted art, uncovered graves, and other matters, it's difficult for us to imagine a time when so little was said.

But I believe the silence wasn't only about the world being unwilling to listen. It also related to lingering fears induced during the Holocaust, and the way survivors understandably carried those fears with them ever after.

Silence was a method of survival during the war and became a way of life in peace as well, at least when the survivors stepped outside their own circles. In effect, they sought a kind of anonymity in the aftermath of their terrors, generally not revealing their pasts as those who suffered during the Holocaust, except to each other. The survivors in Skokie who didn't come out until provoked by neo-Nazi Frank Collin were but one example of the long-lasting silence.

"They were afraid of being identified," Wiesel agreed, but he referred not only to a fear of being recognized as survivors in their newfound countries. He referenced a deeper fear rooted in their experiences.

"Remember one thing," he said to me. "When we stood in line in camp and the SS would come, the worst thing would be to catch his eye. So we looked, but you couldn't close your eyes. You only hoped that he wouldn't stop and look at your eyes: to be seen and to be remarked upon, which means to be marked, to be singled out. Just to be seen is dangerous.

"And therefore, instinctively, better not to be known. At that time, to survive a moment—a moment—was already a victory. Some victory: a moment. The survivors were afraid."

The survivors had learned that looking away, disappearing into the background, staying anonymous, remaining silent, had helped them live through the war and often became a survival strategy afterward. Thus my mother's near-total silence about her past.

Many survivors, perhaps most, changed their names in America, Australia, Israel, wherever they landed, creating new identities for themselves. Psychiatric studies assert that many survivors put their old personalities away as well, or tried to, in effect "splitting" into a new, outer persona and an inner, past personality buried out of view. They often invented, as I mentioned earlier, what Dr. Joel Sadavoy called a "false self."

That traumatically induced persona "meets the world successfully when supported by life circumstances such as stable marriage, having and raising children, immersion in activities and friendship, work and good health," wrote Dr. Sadavoy. "But the traumatically affected part of the self lies vulnerable beneath the surface; emotions and thoughts are waiting to be tripped."

Silence was a way of avoiding that trip wire. This is exactly what happened to my mother, who was so silent about her past that my sister and I knew almost nothing of her secret childhood. To discuss this subject with us surely would have been unbearable for her.

"Because to talk to one's own [family] means to bring pain," as Wiesel analyzed it. "Also to admit victimhood. It's not a nice word, victimhood."

By staying silent, "they simply felt safer," said Wiesel. "They didn't trust humanity. Nor did I."

And yet Wiesel responded differently than many survivors, refusing, for instance, to change his name. Along these lines, his protagonist in *The Forgotten*, Malkiel Rosenbaum—a son of a survivor—decries how Jews' names were erased as they entered America.

"If you knew the transformations Ellis Island has perpetrated!" he says in speaking aloud at the grave of his grandfather, who is also his namesake. "Slomowicz became Salvatore if the immigration officer was Italian, Slocum if he was Anglo-Saxon or Irish. Isaac didn't sound right? They made it Irving."

Elie Wiesel clung to his name, and through the publication of *Night* announced his past as a survivor. Moreover, by actively encouraging other survivors to tell their stories, publish their books, and otherwise shatter the silence, he offered an alternative to masking one's identity.

"No matter what, I felt I am not going to give up what I am, just like that," he said. "I am not going to give up what I am. They took everything away from me. But not more. The main thing is you want to cling to something that cannot be changed. What cannot be changed is your past. Which means I cling to my past, I glorify it, I celebrate it, going back to David."

For Wiesel, "Running away [from the past] is impossible and unworthy. Therefore, the only thing to do is, on the contrary, to be authentic with yourself."

Remembering and celebrating the past—with all its tragedies and pain—was Wiesel's way of adhering to his identity and ending the silence.

But there were other ways as well, and one that was unmistakable in my parents and uncounted other survivors I have known—Wiesel included—is work. My father officially retired from the bakery at age sixty-five and continued to toil there part time until his illness struck at age sixty-seven. My mother cooked and cleaned constantly while my father was alive; after my father died, when she lived alone in our little Skokie home, she said she did three loads of laundry a day and went grocery shopping several times a week. My mother's aunt Irene worked as a paralegal on Holocaust restitution cases until she was nearly ninety.

This ferocious commitment to work, too, was born of the years of terror, Wiesel said. For those caught up in the Holocaust, working was a way "not to feel useless," he said. "There was fear, during the war, to be useless. And the fear survived."

To not have work papers in the ghettos, of course, meant death was imminent. To not be old enough or strong enough to work when entering Auschwitz or the other camps was to be put in the wrong line in the "selections" that led to the gas chambers.

Once again, fears created during the war resonated ever after.

But I believe there was another reason my parents and other survivors worked so hard into old age: to try to keep terrible memories at bay. As we age, research has shown, we tend to look back at our lives, taking stock.

"The trouble is that in the process of reviewing one's life, as the memories are restored . . . and are owned up to (in other words, in the process of the return of the repressed), the individual experiences pain," wrote the psychiatrist and survivor Dr. Henry Krystal. Those memories, added Krystal, "are so intense, threatening and painful that one must ward them off by deadening oneself or abort the process by escaping into denial."

Work offered an escape for survivors, it seems to me. But Wiesel rejected this idea that survivors used work to try to keep bad memories away.

"Not really," he said. "I think somehow you could not suppress those memories. You can cover them up a little bit, but they always come back."

Instead, he cited another reason so many survivors, like himself, toiled into an exalted age.

"For them, every moment is grace," he said. "They know that they could have died a tragic death, like others. Since they didn't, we must justify our lives, every day, every hour, every minute, whatever we do."

The survivors, Wiesel maintained, worked to make every moment of life carry meaning. Though the very fact that they survived seems to me to have been meaningful enough.

11

Moments of Grace

Even if we cannot reconcile what happened with plausible explanations, we are not helpless, said Wiesel. We can act—not to save those who no longer can be saved but to tell the world what happened to them. To invoke the power of words.

"The main thing is that the stories are told," said Wiesel. "We cannot say, 'Once we didn't know.' The survivors spoke. We cannot go back. Therefore, we must tell the story. Therefore, there is hope that the story cannot happen again. Therefore, history has a meaning."

That meaning is apparent to me every time I visit my mother, for whom the Holocaust has not ended but, rather, continues. But all the storytelling and intellectualizing about what happened sometimes seems to me like just so many words: sentences and paragraphs and chapters in books appear slight alongside the horrors of real deeds and tragic consequences.

"If you tell the story well, then it has its own lesson," countered Wiesel. "And the lesson is: Next time, stop before it's too late. Stop. There's always a moment when the killer can be stopped. Because we stopped him or because society stopped him or because he himself stops. Because and because and because, but there is a moment. And that moment is yours."

It seemed to me that Wiesel was saying that knowing the story and telling it are not enough. What matters is how you tell the story, and where and when and to whom and to what effect. This is what brings real purpose and action to what otherwise are only words. As Wiesel has written, "Words can sometimes, in moments of grace, attain the quality of deeds."

When the words we write and speak are delivered in dangerous times and places, they can carry real power, he was saying. In these instances, they are more than just words. Morality, Wiesel said to me many times, can be expressed as the willingness to say no when it counts most.

"That's the test: to say no," said Wiesel. "But that goes very, very far. No to God? Why? If God is a God who tells me to kill other people in his name, I would say, 'No, sorry, so in that case you are not my God.' Which means, again, it always comes back to: you can say no."

Had more people uttered that word as Hitler ascended, history would have unfolded in quite another way, I said to Wiesel.

"It would have been a different world," Wiesel agreed. "But, again, at that time, civilization was such that it was impossible to say no. Can you imagine, in the SS, when you say no? You would be shot."

Unfortunately, I told Wiesel, many said yes, and with enthusiasm.

"They said yes, and they believed in it," he said. "And the word that you mentioned—*enthusiasm*—unfortunately. Some were enthusiastically murderers. When you see sometimes in movies—documentaries—the ecstasy on their faces, on the young faces. Ecstasy! My God, ecstasy.

"Which means that they were simply misled, miseducated. They thought they were doing the right thing. They thought that they were doing the most beautiful thing. They were convinced. When you read the text, you see that they really believed that they were not only following the sense of history, but they were following the sense of what is good and noble in history."

And too few said no when it counted most. Wiesel, I believe, was trying to say that now it is our turn to tell the stories, to stand up, to say no when necessary. Not simply to illuminate the past but alter what happens next. That's when words have palpable power. That's when our stories—the stories we've heard and witnessed and pieced together from the fragments our parents told us—change history in the making.

"The student could ask, When should we have stopped?" said Wiesel, continuing his discussion of that potentially explosive word, *no*. "And there the answer is immediately. Just immediately. The very first time when you realize—in class, for example, when the teacher tells you it's right to kill one hundred people because they were Jews. You have to say, 'Not for me. If that is humanity, I don't want to be part of it.' Right away. Don't give it even a second chance."

Speak out at the moment when it matters most, Wiesel was saying. That's what I believe Wiesel urged us to do now, in the aftermath of what happened.

That theme resonates in Wiesel's writings, as in *The Forgotten*, about a man—Elhanan ben Malkiel—whose precious memory is being stolen by Alzheimer's disease. He feels this is happening to him because once, when he witnessed a heinous crime against humanity, he looked away, instead of saying no.

"I forgot our precepts, our laws, that require an individual to struggle against evil wherever it appears," Elhanan says to his son. "I forgot that we can never simply remain spectators, we have no right to stand aside, to keep silent, to let the victim fight the aggressor alone."

The moral burden is on us, Wiesel was saying, to act and to speak out. It's all part of what Wiesel discussed earlier about witnesses.

"Survivors are witnesses, but anyone who listens to a witness becomes one," he said. "So those who read us, those who hear us, really make the witnesses ours. Here and there it always happened that one of them—a student—gets up in the middle of my class: 'Professor, trust us, we shall be your witnesses.' This is the greatest reward one can get."

We, the second generation—and the third and fourth and those who come after—are now the witnesses, Wiesel maintained, and what we say can compel action, can change the future, if spoken well and in what Wiesel calls moments of grace.

But it's not only the heirs of survivors who can use past histories to remake future ones, he said. It's anyone who hears us, anyone who's in Wiesel's class—anyone, really, open to facing the darkest tales of the past and applying them in the present, especially at critical moments.

I mentioned to Wiesel another occasion for speaking up and saying no: when the most frequently uttered and injurious Holocaust cliché emerges. You know, the one asking why the Jews of Europe didn't resist, why they went to the slaughter like sheep.

I always argue that they did resist, and not only in the famous case of the Warsaw ghetto uprising. They also resisted by trying to live, whether by escaping the ghetto the way my mother did at age eleven or by surviving the terrors of Buchenwald the way my father and Wiesel did as young men. Anyone who survived did so because he or she resisted, I argue, rejecting the widely accepted myth of Jewish acceptance of annihilation.

Wiesel took my point a step further. He asserted that asking why Jews in Europe didn't resist is the wrong question. The true question is: Why *did* they resist? Why did those who rose up in Warsaw and other ghettos across the continent dare to do so, even though they knew the foremost military machine in Europe could crush them and did? Why did they fight to live when an entire society had determined that they be killed?

"After the war, especially in Palestine, then in Israel, the question was, Why didn't you resist?" he said. "It began during the Eichmann trial. Why didn't you resist? Go explain. When you had the mightiest army in the world surrounding the ghetto. What could you do? What could you do?

"There was resistance in the Warsaw ghetto and in other ghettos. But real organized resistance could have been done—if they had helped us. But nobody came to help us."

But wasn't the desire to live itself a form of resistance?

"I could go further," he answered. "Trying to believe is a form of resistance. Trying to pray and believe in God."

And perhaps it was not Jews who were led like sheep but Germans. Weren't they the ones who followed Hitler's demagoguery into genocide?

"How do you explain the fact that a whole people in Germany overnight let itself become sheep who did the murdering and the slaughtering?" Wiesel said during the question-and-answer session at a talk in Wisconsin in 1966.

Too few dared to say no in what might have been moments of grace.

12

How Do We Speak of This?

The word itself, and all it signified, was radioactive to me for most of my life. Now, after all I've read and written and seen as my mother became lost in her past, the reverse seems to be true. I say the word too easily, as if it references simply another chapter in history rather than the source of my family's tragedy and that of millions of others. I know that this subject stands apart from everything else, and so I wonder if avoidance of the *H* word showed more respect toward its meaning.

Which draws us to a fundamental question: How do we speak and write of the Holocaust?

It so happens that Wiesel was among the first to use the word in this context. Why did he invoke *Holocaust*, a term so fraught that generations avoided it?

When I asked, he said that he was writing an essay on the binding of Isaac, when God asked Abraham, "'Bring me your son in a fiery offering,' which is called *olah*, which means 'in fire,' as in Holocaust," said Wiesel.

He went on to explain that he considered fire the closest metaphor he could conceive for events that consumed millions. That *Holocaust* became the universally accepted English-language term for these events suggests Wiesel made a potent choice. The word entered common parlance "because it's evocative," he said. "It means *victim*, and it means *fire*, and these two terms, of course, are part of the territory, of the vocabulary, defining the tragedy."

Or at least as much as language is able to do. But has overuse of the word numbed us to the terror that it was originally designed to convey? Wiesel said he developed reservations about how the world employs the term. Its intended meaning and connotations have been diluted and diminished through overuse, misuse, and trivialization. We both had heard sports announcers speaking of a holocaust for the losing side. A sacrilege.

"All of a sudden, everything was a holocaust, everything—it was on TV," said Wiesel, lamenting the ubiquity of a descriptor now applied haphazardly for events major and minor but no longer reserved for an exclusive moment in history.

"Look, you can simply say *catastrophe*, yes," said Wiesel, in suggesting alternatives. "*Tragedy*—absolutely, absolutely. Monstrous tragedy. But some words are copyrighted by the events themselves, OK? They are. Be careful. And, as always, people read me, but they don't listen to me."

Or they listen too well, the world having embraced the word Wiesel turned to early on and, in so doing, reducing its shattering power. The problem has gone so far that Wiesel had taken to qualifying his own usage, referring to "what we so poorly call the Holocaust," as he often said to me. Or he bypassed the term altogether, speaking simply of "the Event—with a capital *E*."

Speaking and writing of the Holocaust, of course, is a challenge that reaches far beyond our increasing insensitivity to a single word. The term is but the gateway to a subject that brings anguish to anyone directly touched by it and to others as well. To try to address these events poses insurmountable problems, even for Wiesel, whose writings nonetheless have cast so much light on this subject.

"I rarely have a good feeling about my writing," said Wiesel, speaking specifically of his prose on the subject of the Holocaust. "It depends what, of course. But let's say vital, or vitally important, is if I write about that war and that Event and that suffering and everything about it, I always feel it's not right. It's still not there. It's not perfect."

Rarely, added Wiesel, "do I have a feeling: 'Ah, now I found the words.' Again, the words cannot . . ." he said, his voice trailing off. It was as if he were saying, through his ensuing silence, that in this instance words are inadequate even to describe their own inadequacy.

All of which begs a question: Why do we even try? If Wiesel is right that language cannot articulate what happened, and if he is correct that anyone who was not there cannot understand—and surely he must be correct in both cases—then why try to write or speak of this? Why indulge in an effort that by Wiesel's own estimation cannot succeed?

The reason may have to do with another, seemingly contradictory belief that Wiesel often referenced in our conversations: that new witnesses must be created so that they can tell the story and generate still more witnesses. In effect, Wiesel seemed to be standing at the nexus of two opposed positions: the failure of words to express what happened and the necessity of continuing to express it.

I posed this paradox to him.

"What is the alternative?" he asked. "Not to write? If I could find another way. So not to write? And yet you must. With the doubts and with the questions, you must write."

Even if language has failed us?

"Failed to say what?" asked Wiesel. "To say something that cannot be said?"

The failure, he seemed to be saying, was not really a failure of language, nor of our attempts to harness it, but of humanity itself. Language is simply our means of coming to terms with that larger failure, a quixotic but essential attempt to explain the unexplainable.

"Logically I should have given up on language," said Wiesel, amplifying the point.

"First of all, the killers also used language. Some of them actually were very erudite and cultivated and educated men and women. And they also read Goethe and Fichte and they listened to Beethoven and Bach. If they did it, how can I believe in the same things they believed in?" Meaning language, literature, and music, among other things.

Clearly we can't relinquish these components of civilization simply because they were co-opted by Nazis. Language can be redeemed, Wiesel said, and the quest to do so was worth pursuing, even if it might not prevail.

"With God's grace, I may find the right words," Wiesel said, hoping for a turn of events that he believed has not yet occurred. "So why should I give up? Why should I deprive my students or my readers from the language they use, simply because the killers are the ones who used it?"

There's another, more personal reason to write of these events despite the obstacles: the model of those who wrote under dire circumstances. Emanuel Ringelblum and colleagues documented the horrors of the Warsaw ghetto in real time, even though he and most of the others did not survive the war and live to see their words read and known by anyone. Presciently they buried their writings beneath the wreckage of the ghetto, one batch of their precious texts discovered in September 1946, another in December 1950. The authors died, but their words lived.

Similarly a few notebooks hidden amid the ashes of Birkenau—such as the diary of Leib Langfus—were found decades later, the near dead having documented their final observations in the midst of their destruction. And Shimon Dubnow, a revered Jewish historian, is believed to have proclaimed aloud before being executed in the Riga ghetto, "Write—and record" (in Yiddish, "*shrayb—un farshrayb*").

If they believed in writing and speaking, so must we, said Wiesel.

"So how can I dare to say, 'I am better than you, and therefore I am not writing'?" he asked, in light of these examples and others. If the victims found hope in language, even in the hours before their deaths, how can we not?

Wiesel interpreted his great difficulty in getting *Night* published and its long period of obscurity to the magnitude of the events it chronicled and to the world's inability to absorb them. In effect, at least a generation needed to pass before the public at large realized that it needed to learn about the Holocaust.

The turning points, said Wiesel, came in Israel during the Eichmann trial, which in 1961 revisited the horrors of past events, and the Six-Day War in 1967, which—until its stunningly swift conclusion—suggested that genocidal disaster was on the verge of occurring again.

In the United States, I believe the breakthrough came a decade later, with the aforementioned 1978 TV broadcast of *Holocaust*, an ABC-TV miniseries, which for the first time put the subject where most American discourse takes place: popular culture.

In the decades that followed, Wiesel's *Night* has been studied world-wide as a startling perspective on an event that its author considered indefinable. Why did *Night* capture so many readers? What did Wiesel put in its pages that gave millions insight into what its author deemed impenetrable events?

How did Wiesel, in other words, find a way of speaking and writing of the Holocaust that reached across so many decades, generations, and continents?

"I swear to you, I don't know," said Wiesel, as if mystified by the global embrace of the words he wrote. "I have published sixty books, and the others are all jealous of *Night*. They come to haunt me in my dreams. My other books are as good. It's luck."

If so, it clearly came at a steep price. But of course it was much more than luck. For starters, it was the experiences that those words reanimated—the tragic, hard-won knowledge that Wiesel brought to his text—that eventually made *Night* required reading. It wasn't only the poetic lyricism of Wiesel's prose but the events they soberly illuminated, from the ominous opening pages set in Wiesel's hometown of Sighet to the tragedies of Auschwitz and Buchenwald.

If, as Wiesel has said, "words can sometimes, in moments of grace, attain the quality of deeds," the words in *Night* became a remarkable deed: the opening of a pathway into the Holocaust for those who were not there.

But when I suggested to Wiesel that anyone is lucky not to have his knowledge of this subject—that the Holocaust is one area of study in which no one wants personal experience or expertise—he surprised me by disagreeing. Though gently.

"I'm not so sure," he said. "Since it happened, I feel that it's right that I should be a part of it. Since it happened. But I would have given anything in the world that it didn't happen."

This was a surprising observation. Wiesel said that if the Holocaust were going to happen, he needed to belong to it, to experience it, to witness it, to present its narrative to the rest of us. His writing and his fate were intertwined, so far as he was concerned, and perhaps this explains the lasting power of his way of writing and speaking of the Holocaust. He wrote not as an accidental witness but as one whose destiny—by virtue of his Jewish identity and the time and place in which he lived—was to be caught up in the Holocaust and later to attempt to describe it.

From that perspective, perhaps Wiesel tells us something valuable about how to address this subject: as if it is our sacred duty to grapple with an event that we would have given everything to have prevented. As if we should want to embrace this most tragic of stories because of who we are.

Furthermore, Wiesel said that the ideas and imagery and emotions rising up from the thousands of pages he has written carry a mysterious power of their own, apart from what he did to put them there.

"I know that the words are inadequate—all the words are," he said. "But nevertheless, I write them. I think the great mystery of life is to be able to put one word to another. And that everything is mystery—even the silence separating the words is mystery."

Those silences rang out eloquently in *Night*, not only in the silences between the words in this slender volume but also in what was left unsaid in it. Repeatedly Wiesel avoided exposition, as in the aftermath of his father's death in Buchenwald—where Wiesel himself and my father also very nearly expired.

"I shall not describe my life during that period," Wiesel wrote in *Night*. "It no longer mattered. Since my father's death, nothing mattered to me anymore."

This was Wiesel's way of speaking of the Holocaust—telegraphically, compactly, with much left unstated and with utmost respect to those who no longer could speak for themselves.

"Two of my older sisters survived," Wiesel said to me, in developing this thought. "I never talked with them about it, except certain occasions."

And then only circumspectly. Wiesel told me that he never asked his surviving sisters what their mother and other sister said during the selection at Auschwitz, moments before their executions. He could not violate something so sacred, and in that act he taught us something about how we should treat such matters. With reverence and, sometimes, with respectful silence.

I have come to believe that the stories of the Holocaust can be expressed in many different ways, and not only with words on the page. My parents and all the other survivors told their tales, too, to their children in ways intended and not. My mother's near-total silence on the subject represented her harrowing testimony, expressed in her avoidance.

Like the mysterious silence that Wiesel detected in the spaces between his words, my mother's quiet spoke a great deal about what the events had done to her and how hard she had tried to distance herself from them. When the terrors of her childhood returned late in life, her autobiography became more readily discerned. My father's recurrent insomnia and raging outbursts were his way of reacting to what happened to him—not in a speech or a book but in private gestures and succinct references for a small yet crucial audience: my mother, my sister, and I, who lived with him.

My parents and others did not have Wiesel's literary tools for addressing the Holocaust, but they found their own ways of telling their stories. Many decades later, I finally began to hear them and write them.

The goal, said Wiesel, was to make sure that the killers will not "sleep well," as he put it.

And he feels we must not either.

And so we write and speak.

13

The Art of Inventing Hope

And yet the genocide continues, as if the world has learned nothing from the Holocaust. Mass killing predicated on identity rages around the globe, from the massacres by ISIS across Syria, Iraq, and Europe to slayings of Ukrainians near the Russian border to internecine slaughters in Africa and beyond. It seems impossible to sustain hope in the face of this, especially after what happened to Wiesel's family and mine and so many others.

As Wiesel might put it: If the world has not learned its lessons from the Holocaust by now, when will it?

I asked Wiesel how it is possible to find hope amid all of this.

He began his answer by recalling words he delivered at the United Nations on January 24, 2005, at a special session of the General Assembly marking sixty years since the Nazi death camps were liberated. Until that anniversary, "the United Nations had never held such a high-level remembrance of the Holocaust," reported the *New York Times*. This was a signal event, and it resonated deeply with Wiesel.

"A few years ago, I was invited to address the General Assembly," Wiesel remembered. "I called my lecture 'Will the World Ever Learn?' And I gave the answer: 'No, because it hasn't learned.' Otherwise, how was one to explain Rwanda and Cambodia? And here we are, we are still here, the witnesses are still giving their testimony. And if we haven't changed the world, who will and who can?"

In his speech, Wiesel cited the world's indifference. He pointed out that disaster might have been averted if the West had responded when Hitler subsumed Czechoslovakia and Austria; or if America and Britain had opened their doors to more souls hoping to flee Central and Eastern Europe; or if the Allies had obliterated the railways leading to the concentration camps. If and if and if.

And Wiesel implored the United Nations not to allow such apathy to triumph again.

"The Jewish witness speaks of his people's suffering as a warning," he told the General Assembly. "He sounds the alarm so as to prevent these things being done. He knows that for the dead it is too late; for them, abandoned by God and betrayed by humanity, victory came much too late. But it is not too late for today's children, ours and yours. It is for their sake alone that we bear witness."

But all of these testimonies, by Wiesel and others, appear to have changed very little when it comes to death by identity.

"This is what makes me so pessimistic," Wiesel told me, using a word I did not expect to encounter from a man as hopeful as he generally seemed to be.

But Wiesel viewed pessimism differently than I expected. To me, pessimism is an ending, a presumption of defeat, a kind of resignation. In a way, it's the natural conclusion, a kind of logical extension of so much bleak history.

To Wiesel, however, it's something quite different: a beginning, a provocation, a call to action. Yes, he's pessimistic, he conceded, "but it's an active pessimism. Not to give up. Because of genocide, you must do more, you must work harder, rather than say, 'Since it hasn't helped, forget it.'"

In effect, Wiesel was wringing a kind of hope from a forlorn landscape, willfully believing we must do more precisely because everything we have done to date has yielded so little. Nurturing an "active pessimism," as Wiesel called it, suggested aspiration.

Still, I wondered exactly what he meant by this curious term, an oxymoron of a sort I'd never encountered.

"Active pessimism is pessimism that therefore moves you to action," he said, offering an explanation of a concept of his own devising.

"The other view actually says, 'Ach, since it's so terrible, what can I do?'

"The active one says, 'Oh, therefore I can do something. And even if I can do nothing, I will do it anyway, just to prove that I'm doing it.'"

Taking action even when you think it may be futile—especially if you think it will be futile—was not only Wiesel's definition of *active pessimism* but also, I believe, his statement of hope amid sorrow. When the quest is failing, he seemed to be saying, we need to work that much harder, not only to try to effect change but also as a statement of who we are.

The world may not listen, genocide may not slow or stop, but we must prove—if only to ourselves—that we will not quietly accept it. We will not indulge in the indifference that made the Holocaust possible. In effect, we create hope by pushing forward in the face of failure. The more that genocide continues, the more energy we should expend against it, not less, Wiesel was saying.

"The only thing to do is to try to protest, which I do," said Wiesel, in expanding on his theme of quixotically speaking out amid tides of genocide. "Sometimes I say I've done nothing else," he added, perhaps acknowledging how little his efforts and those of so many others seem to have changed the course of events (though surely he has altered thinking among uncounted students and readers).

"All of these killings and killings and killings which are going on, so long, and still going on, in all kinds of places—how can it go on?" he asked. "And therefore at times I would say, 'Ah, look at me. I also had reasons to go and do terrible things afterward. I didn't. The human grandeur is *not* to give in to that. To say, 'I have my own way. Why don't you choose that?'"

Holocaust survivors like Wiesel and my parents, in other words, chose not to extend the cycle of killing in the name of revenge but chose hope instead. If they could find reason to continue in the face of their incalculable losses, how could the rest of us not follow their example?

How could we give up hope when they did not? Hope survives in their example. In effect, the survivors did not give in to a hate they might have been inclined to pursue, reaching instead for something better.

This crucial choice emerges in Wiesel's novel *The Fifth Son*, in which a son of survivors is very nearly consumed by hate and hopes of revenge, traveling to Germany to find and confront the man—the Angel of Death—responsible for killings in his father's hometown.

"In truth, I am drawn to hate," the son writes in a letter to his murdered brother. "I am drawn to the Angel. I need to hate, to hate him. I look upon hate as a solution for the present: it blinds, it intoxicates; in short it keeps one distracted."

And yet, when the survivor's son is within striking distance of the killer, he turns away from killing.

"Once the words had been exchanged, I could leave," he says in *The Fifth Son*. "The Angel no longer provoked in me either hatred or thirst for revenge. I had disturbed the pattern of his existence, renewed his memory, spoiled his future joys, that was enough for me."

Words, rather than revenge, would be his balm.

"I shall speak," he said. "I shall tell the tale."

This was Wiesel's way, too, of defusing hate: through writing, speaking, educating.

"Hatred is a disease," Wiesel said to me. "And if you don't stop it somewhere, it continues. Therefore, at one point, you will hate the other person, and then you discover the other person in yourself. Some small things: the way he or she [holds a] fork. Other more important things: the way he or she reacts to a book, to a film, to a concert."

Hatred, Wiesel seemed to be saying, only intensifies as the hater sees aspects of himself in those he hates. Or as Wiesel's protagonist put it in *The Fifth Son*, "Such are the dynamics of hate: it overflows. . . . All hate becomes self-hate."

To Wiesel, hatred perpetuates itself.

"There are so many reasons for hatred," he said, "that it's almost a miracle that hatred is not spreading even faster, stronger." Here, perhaps, was another instance of Wiesel's active pessimism, the man finding a sliver of optimism even in the notion that hatred had not metastasized more quickly than we know it already has.

Perhaps this is a form of hope. And to Wiesel, hope is essential to life.

"Without hope," he said, "there could be no human links. If I meet you, there is a hope, maybe without words, but hope that something good can come out of our encounter, or there would be no encounter."

But what of despair, the opposite of hope, a state of mind the Holocaust seems to have mandated? Despair seems to me to be a much more natural outcome of these events. Wiesel—who told me that his mission as teacher, writer, and witness is designed, above all, "to give hope"—said that despair is not the answer. It is the question.

"If despair is the answer, where do we go?" he asked. "What can we build on? What can we begin? If I know from the beginning that it all leads to despair, how can we go on?

"It's difficult enough to think that we are all mortal, that at the end we all die. I try to teach my students and my readers the art of listening and the art of inventing hope even when there is no hope. Let despair take care of itself. I believe much more in hope."

But for some people, despair is indeed the answer. I have seen it. It is what their losses and pain inexorably have led them to, and how can we blame them? We must respect their despair, I said to Wiesel.

He disagreed.

"First of all, despair of what?" he asked. "Despair of life? Despair of tomorrow? Despair of the future? What is despair? Despair is more than a lack of hope. It's a choice. Now I choose to despair, which means to give up, to give in, totally. I'm no longer worthy of living another hour. That's the real despair. That we don't accept.

"If you are a believing Jew, God is the ultimate judge. He is the one who says, 'OK, that's it, the end.' These words can be written only by God, and not by any human being. That's what the Jewish faith believes and wants me to believe. And therefore, despair really is an act.

"We had a choice [after the Holocaust]. We could have chosen despair, becoming anarchists—nihilists, in the philosophical terms:

'Don't talk to me about all that. I have seen it. We have seen it. The worst things we have seen that men and women of culture have done. How could they? With PhDs in their pockets. How could they?' But they could, and they did.

"What is despair? Despair: 'I don't want to read any more books. Enough. What can they teach me?'

"Instead, I read more and more and more and more and more. Despair is never an answer. And if it is, it's the wrong answer.

"I would say, the survivor says to his friends and to his children and to his companions, 'Look, if we despaired, we wouldn't be here. It was so easy, just so easy to give in, to give up. It was the easiest thing in the world, because that was a temptation. Like the Angel of Death would say, 'Come on. Stop it. You can. Stop it. Don't you see tomorrow will be another day of suffering, another day of hunger, another day of humiliation? Stop it. Come on. Death can be a solution.'"

But Wiesel and the other survivors—as well as those who struggled to survive but did not—resisted, out of hope. How else to explain their perseverance during the Holocaust and in the challenges that followed? The battle for hope emerged lucidly in the pages of Wiesel's novel *The Gates of the Forest*, in which a Holocaust survivor haunted by his experiences eventually, painstakingly finds his way back to hope.

"Know then that all of us have our ghosts," the survivor says to his wife, as he resolves to embrace both his tragic past and a more hopeful future. "They come and go at will, breaking open doors, never shutting them tight; they bear different names. We mustn't let ourselves be seduced by their promises. . . . They'll continue to haunt us, but we must fight them. It will be a bigger, austere, obstinate battle. The struggle to survive will begin here, in this room, where we are sitting. Whether or not the Messiah comes doesn't matter; we'll manage without him. It is because it is too late that we are commanded to hope."

Indeed, the Messiah was too late. And still Wiesel believed that Jewish tradition urges us to hope.

In Wiesel's *The Fifth Son*, a rabbi asserts, "Our tradition forbids despair. Even as the sword touches your throat, turn your thoughts toward heaven: divine intervention is as quick as the blink of an eye."

Wiesel insisted that, for Jews, hope is more than an aspiration. It's an imperative.

"We are ordered to hope," he said to me. "That's very powerful. We are ordered to hope. Which means if you lose hope, you commit a sin. You are ordered to go on clinging to hope, even when there is none, you must go on clinging to hope."

But how was it even possible to invent hope—to use Wiesel's phrase—after the Holocaust, even if so commanded? Where did Wiesel and my parents and other survivors find the wherewithal to conjure hope where there was none to be found and no reason to believe it could be?

The answers surely vary from one person to the next, but Wiesel said there are commonalities in these shared experiences as well. By way of example, he pointed to what he considered the first method of finding hope after the Holocaust: in community.

"Hope is not something that I can have if I am alone—the fact is that I was not alone immediately after the war, but at the same time I was more alone than ever before," said Wiesel, pointing to yet another Holocaust paradox. For although survivors found one another after the war, each had lost most of those who had been close to them.

They were alone together.

"But I was not the only one to feel like that," said Wiesel. "We were together. The others also felt like that. We were together. And that gives us something."

The survivors thus had a basis for starting to rebuild hope. As they scattered to countries around the world, they clung to one another, surely to find safety in numbers and to be with the only ones who understood what happened but also, perhaps, to find hope.

"We were four hundred that came to the OSE [children's rescue society] from Buchenwald," recalled Wiesel, citing the first bonds he established after the war. "One hundred of them were religious, and I was one of them, as I told you. So we had much in common. A religious group is a community. Which means every morning we have to get up to pray. Not we had to pray—we wanted to get up to pray.

"The main thing was for us, for instance, at what point do we say Kaddish?" asked Wiesel, referring to the Hebraic prayer for the dead. "You're supposed to say Kaddish a whole year after the death of a parent. When does it begin? For us it was a difficult thing," added Wiesel, since so many knew not when their parents were killed, or even—as in my mother's case—where.

"But we said Kaddish," continued Wiesel. "Kaddish, you know, is a very special prayer. The word *death* does not figure in it, yet this is the prayer for the dead.

"So the hope actually came from each other. The fact that we could sing together and celebrate the Sabbath together and try to pick up where we had left off, and that there is a continuity."

Wiesel said that he and the others found a beginning of hope in each other, in their shared losses, in their common aloneness, in their daunting futures. I believe this is what my parents and so many other survivors found in Skokie—a link to those who had been through the same events, even if the details of each story were different. Without necessarily saying so, they drew hope from each other, because they had lived, and they did so all over the world, converging in places such as Skokie and Brooklyn, Los Angeles and Miami, Tel Aviv and Sydney.

And they found hope in one other place that wasn't geographical but was surely more important to them: in us, their sons and daughters.

"First of all, you were our hope—we had children," said Wiesel. "Logically it was crazy, for Jews who went through what we went through to have children. I knew people who refused to get married. They said, 'What for? Why bring Jewish children to a world that doesn't want them?' I knew them.

"The answer was, of course, that we had incidents in history—not quite like the Holocaust—one thousand years ago, and we wrote that our sages had that problem. But they overruled. They said, 'No, life must go on.'"

And so it did, the survivors heroically rebuilding families and, in so doing, hope. From loss and despair they created lives and futures. My parents never spoke in such exalted terms. They never referenced hope or history, biblical commands or Jewish survival, but their actions demonstrated their point of view. They had children and grandchildren. They perpetuated life.

They showed the outcome of hope.

14

On Faith

How did Wiesel and the other survivors cling to belief? How was it possible to hold on to faith after the Jews of Europe were abandoned by the world—and as Wiesel has said, by God? Surely everyone touched by these events, particularly survivors and their heirs, grapples with this discord: How does one honor faith in light of what happened and what continues to happen?

Wiesel would not tell me how to resolve this problem. To the contrary, "I cannot pass judgment," he said. "I have my way, but they have absolutely the right to choose theirs, and I must respect."

But even though he would not provide a specific answer on how to maintain faith, he offered a way of *thinking* about faith in the face of genocide. As he explained it, we constantly struggle between what we try to believe and the grim events that have occurred (and continue to).

"How can one not?" said Wiesel, acknowledging, as he often has, that faith was—and is—severely tested by the Holocaust.

I never asked my father or mother how they maintained their belief after their experiences, but I couldn't help noticing the toll that their pasts had taken on it. My father had been raised in a religious family, recited Hebraic prayers fluently, and performed Jewish rituals meticulously until the war. When he and a surviving brother opened their little bakery in Chicago's Germantown in the 1950s, however, we never so much as walked past a synagogue, let alone visited one.

Even when we moved to Skokie, a kind of shelter for Holocaust survivors in America, we went to temple only on the High Holy Days, never on the Sabbath or any other time. My dad made sure I attended Hebrew school and that I had a bar mitzvah, but his own relationship to the practice of religion seemed far removed from the piety of his youth.

My mother had no religious training whatsoever in the brief years of her innocence, before the Russians invaded her town when she was eight years old. During the war, she had learned Christian prayers to survive, she once told me. Decades later, when we went to temple in Skokie, Hebraic customs were utterly foreign to her, my mother simply mouthing the phonetic pronunciations of texts in the prayer books that must have looked to her like hieroglyphics.

Yet both my parents told me they believed in God. Even so, it was easy to see that their faith—or least my father's—had been injured by the past. They never articulated any of this to me, but the words Wiesel offered may have summed up their feelings on the subject.

"You can struggle outside or inside" religion, he said to me. "I prefer to do it inside faith. If it's outside, it's finished, goodbye God. Finished. Right? And there is no problem anymore. And problems are part of my existence, of my consciousness, and of my life. I prefer that."

It's the battle with faith, not the easy acceptance of it, that seemed to matter most to Wiesel and perhaps applied to my parents and many other survivors as well. Like Wiesel, my parents continued to believe, staying inside faith, though just barely. Wiesel had expressed this explicitly in conversation, accepting the difficulties of faith in the face of the Holocaust rather than either abandoning it or unconditionally accepting it. He chose to examine this contradiction within Judaism rather than outside of it, and I believe that's what my parents and others did, without explicitly saying so. My parents remained Jews but never forgot how much that identity had cost them. In Wiesel's case, he refused to blame religion for the misdeeds of man, and I believe this was true of my parents as well.

"Auschwitz was not an institution that came down from heaven ready-made," Wiesel said to me. "It was made, conceived, thought through by human beings against other human beings. That means I should actually give up, first of all, my faith in humanity, and I should say, 'Go to hell. All your culture, all your philosophical trials, go to hell. If you and your culture could do that, I want nothing to do with it.'

"Is that the answer? We cannot think this way. We live in a society. And then there are children in the world who need to be taught. And there are friends who need to be encouraged. The same thing is with God. Look, I cannot conceive of Auschwitz with God or without God."

Wiesel, like all of us touched by the Holocaust, found himself caught between forces that cannot be reconciled, but he refused to give up his faith in the face of this impasse. At the same time, he clearly could not accept what happened in the context of faith. Instead, he separated faith and the Holocaust, awaiting an explanation on how they can come to terms. If they ever really can.

We of the second generation similarly try to fathom a puzzle: To turn away from Judaism would be to wipe away part of our identity and disrespect our parents' tragic history and the unimaginable loss of their families. Yet clinging to faith after learning about Auschwitz, Buchenwald, and other scenes of terror is not easy.

Wiesel offered a different way of looking at the problem.

"I say to myself, 'Look, my father was religious to the end,'" he said. "My grandfather was religious, my great-grandfather. I cannot betray them. So what do I say? I say, 'OK, in spite of God, I will continue believing in God.'"

This is Wiesel's way: maintaining faith despite events, in part because faith to Wiesel was interwoven with family legacy, as it surely is to most of us.

"Of course it is," said Wiesel. "Each time I make a choice, the choice is somehow related to my own life. And the choice is: How can I not believe? And how can I believe, when I know so much? All of that, of course, is a part of my life story."

We cannot really untangle faith, religion, culture, history, tragedy, and our family biographies. They're interwoven and inseparable and need to be understood whole, in all their complexity, with all their contradictions.

"My generation, maybe a little bit yours, too, could have had all the reasons in the world to give up hope and faith and say, 'Come on, Mr. God, if this is what you want from your people, thank you, have it your way, and leave me alone,'" Wiesel said to me.

"But you don't. It's too easy. And we say, 'Look, we accept all the challenges and all the follies and all the hopes and all the fires and all the defeats, everything. We accept everything, as long as we are a part of the same story.' That's the main thing. We are still part of the same story.

"Somewhere in my own lifetime we have seen Abraham leading his son, or his son leading his father, to the altar," said Wiesel, referring metaphorically to the Holocaust. Just as Abraham's faith was tested by God's command to sacrifice his son, so ours is tested by the incalculable sacrifices of the Holocaust.

We are left to struggle with this enigma, and the only choice is whether to do so with or without faith.

"Exactly," said Wiesel. "Otherwise it's too easy, and who wants to live easy answers? You can find all these things and the opposite, all because our Jewish philosophy is so rich, and it's so rich because of its contradictions."

Wiesel, in other words, accepted the conflicts and the unfathomable questions surrounding faith. This was why he could speak of believing in God in spite of God while also considering himself "inside" of faith. One's doubts, he seemed to be saying, need not interfere with the intensity of one's beliefs.

"Remember, I speak as a Hasid," he said to me, referring to the term for a fervently religious Jew. "What is Hasidism if not the ecstatic expression of Judaism? Religious Judaism.

"You know, we live in a need of ecstasy. What is ecstasy? It's to go beyond. This is what we try to do. Especially you, who studies music," he said, aiming his analysis specifically my way. "What is music, if not that?"

Indeed, like religion, music takes us beyond the corporeal, and its powers cannot be easily explained. I know, for I have spent a career trying. For many, music provides the kind of refuge, comfort, and transcendence that others find in faith. Like religion, at certain extraordinary moments it can take people "beyond." The redemptive climaxes of certain symphonies of Beethoven, the late-period quests of jazz saxophonist John Coltrane, the otherworldly tones of Maurice Ravel's orchestral works, the high-flying scat singing of Ella Fitzgerald all have epitomized the ecstasies that I believe Wiesel found in Hasidism and others perhaps discovered in different realms.

By ecstasy—in religion or music or other endeavors—I believe Wiesel referenced a desire to push beyond the rational, the explainable, the obvious, and to go to another place. To go "always beyond, higher and higher and higher, more and more intense and more and more melodious, but always higher, always higher," as Wiesel put it to me. "It cannot stop trying to go higher. And that is really what we have in ecstasy. And the word in Hebrew, it's very nice: burning on fire. You should learn with burning fire."

Another way of looking at this is to say that to Wiesel, faith was not a noun but a verb—a process, a pursuit. If I and other children of survivors struggle with faith in light of our family histories, that means only that we are partaking in an evolution of thought and emotion that may not have an end point in our lifetimes. Still we strive.

Wiesel did not discount this struggle nor criticize those who reject faith in light of what happened. To the contrary, he acknowledged, accepted, and understood this perspective, at least to judge by his words in *The Gates of the Forest*: "Never despise, never spit at a man who has broken with the faith," says a character in Wiesel's novel. "He is accomplishing his destiny."

But how can Wiesel accept a rejection of the faith for which so many gave so much?

"I respect," he insisted when I asked him about this passage. "Except those who don't respect. Those who speak about anyone else's faith, their opinions, or their commitments [with] disrespect—that I don't accept. Who are we, anyway, to become the other person's judge?"

Wiesel said we cannot judge anyone else's relationship to faith, we can only grapple with our own. He contended that we should view faith as something designed for our own well-being. Faith is for the benefit of the faithful, not for the benefit of God.

As he wrote in *The Gates of the Forest*: "Do you know why God demands that you love him? He doesn't need your love, he can do without it, but you can't."

Or as Wiesel expressed it to me, "Why should God need us? Who are we to really say that God needs us? It's for us."

And what about Mormons who say they posthumously have been converting Jews—including Holocaust survivors—to Mormonism? Whether or not you believe in such postmortem declarations, there's something galling about members of one religion purporting to claim the souls of Jews who were massacred precisely for their own religious identity. How dare they?

"Yeah, I discovered one day that they converted 650,000 victims," said Wiesel. "I laughed, really. I can imagine my grandfather would arrive all of a sudden in heaven, and he will say to me, 'I don't know you—you're not a Mormon!'

"How could they do that and not laugh, really? But then I felt that it's a dangerous business. That's why I protest publicly. They meant well. They said, 'We want to save you. Therefore, thank us. It's for your sake, for your good. You are now Mormons. No more anti-Semites anymore.'"

I told Wiesel that it seemed to me that this is almost the antithesis of Judaism, which actively discourages conversion, or at least puts so many requirements and rituals in the path of anyone who wishes to become Jewish as to serve as a series of hurdles. Wiesel saw these requirements somewhat differently: not as an obstacle but as a statement of purpose.

"Yes," the hurdles are there, said Wiesel, "but it's not only that. We are simply against that. We believe a person should be what he or she is. That's the only reason. You're born a Jew, be a Jew. You want to be a Jew, be a Jew. We don't say that a Jew is better than anyone else and therefore don't become one. Be who you are."

That is the essence of the struggle, isn't it? Being who you are in light of the Holocaust and despite it.

The struggle continues.

15

Can We Forgive?

And now we come to the concept that may be the most fraught: forgiveness. This is a word that many toss around lightly for slights and bruises that indeed can be forgiven. For some events, apologies may be accepted, forgiveness may be possible.

Not for this, however. There is no apology that can be expressed, no atonement that can be delivered in the aftermath of what happened, I believe.

Wiesel took a more nuanced view, saying that for members of the second generation, the idea of forgiveness is an intensely private decision. Children of survivors must come to their own conclusions.

"He or she must decide, because of their relationship with their parents, or their grandparents, or to the memory," said Wiesel. "Some children of survivors, like their parents—or against their parents—say they will never set foot in Germany.

"Others say, 'Why not? If we go there for business, we teach them something.' Both arguments are valid, and who am I to judge if one is better?"

I'd spent most of my life avoiding travel to Germany until a newspaper story took me there. I did not miss the irony of the situation: a journalist who had been avoiding his family's history found himself tracing the provenance of rare violins looted during the Holocaust. The nation evoked no particular emotions in me, though the story surely did.

When I met Germans my age, I wondered what their parents did during the war, while mine were fighting to live. I admired Wiesel's generosity in suggesting that each child of survivors should establish his or her own way of dealing with this place. But hadn't Wiesel himself once criticized Jews who chose to live in Germany after the war?

In a question-and-answer session following a lecture in Wisconsin in 1966, he was asked, "Given the events of the Holocaust, what should be our relationship to the German Jews who went back to Germany?"

Wiesel replied, "I feel ashamed that Jews still live in Germany."

He also said, "Politically I am against the official policy of Jewish leadership and even of Israel—of coexistence with the German people. I know money is needed. I know reparations are important. But somehow I feel terribly embarrassed when I think that we asked the Germans only for money after the war. So I do not go to Germany. I do not want their reparations or their money."

But half a century later, Wiesel's views on Jews in Germany had evolved.

"I changed—that I changed," Wiesel said to me. "Who am I to give them instructions? I am a witness. And in that phrase, I expressed a judgment. Who am I to tell them what to do? What do I know about them? If they felt that their life is better there because they cannot find a job anywhere else, who am I to say no? I still felt I had no right to tell other Jews what to do with their lives.

"Would I be able to do it?" asked Wiesel, referring to the prospect of living in Germany afterward. "I said no. Some people, say, go to Germany to teach. What right do I have to tell them not to? Really. If they want to go and they feel they can and they teach their German students or Jewish students in Germany, go ahead, I'm not your judge. Absolutely. So it changed a little bit."

Despite Wiesel's evolved viewpoint and my own ambivalence, I told him of my admiration of the pianist Arthur Rubinstein, and not only on musical terms. Rubinstein's family in Lodz, Poland, was destroyed in the Holocaust. Afterward, Rubinstein refused to set foot in Germany ever again, regardless of how much German audiences wished to hear one of the greatest concert pianists of the twentieth century or how often German impresarios and orchestras begged him to perform there. No price was high enough. Rubinstein would not forgive.

As for himself, Wiesel expressed a distinctive view of forgiveness. In January 2000, he was invited to address the German parliament, he told me, and he paraphrased what he said, with German president Johannes Rau in attendance:

"Mr. President, Germany has done great things for my people after the war. First, you helped the survivors with money and all kinds of other help. You helped Israel a lot. One thing you have never done: You have never asked the Jewish people for forgiveness. Why haven't you? And why don't you?"

After reciting this soliloquy, Wiesel took a breath and then told me, "You can imagine the silence in the hall."

He was startled, however, to learn that a couple of weeks later, in February, President Rau went to the Knesset in Jerusalem and "for the first and only time asked the Jewish people for forgiveness," said Wiesel.

Indeed, Rau offered these words: "With the people of Israel watching, I bow in humility before those murdered, before those who don't have graves where I could ask them for forgiveness. I am asking for forgiveness for what Germans have done, for myself and my generation, for the sake of our children and our grandchildren, whose future I would like to see alongside the children of Israel."

Yet Wiesel said he personally could not extend absolution.

"I cannot issue a declaration of forgiveness for the whole people," he said to me. "I cannot authorize that. Only the dead could authorize that.

"The only question would be a personal one. Do I, as a person, forgive? No one has ever asked me. What if I were to be stopped, let's say, on the streets of Chicago or New York by a man saying, 'Professor Wiesel, do you remember you were beaten up that day? I did it.'

"Nobody did" offer such an apology, Wiesel said. "So I'm actually in a privileged situation. I don't have to answer that question."

Though, based on Wiesel's comments, it didn't seem difficult to guess what that answer would be.

Wiesel addressed the issue even more pointedly in another context, speaking to students in Wisconsin in 1966.

"I do not think that forgiveness is relevant," he said. "Not forgetting—that is relevant."

Even so, in our conversations he took pains to avoid indicting the entire German culture of the 1930s and '40s for what happened, as I sometimes had done.

"Let's not go that far," Wiesel cautioned me. "Not all Germans believed that Jews should be eradicated. That plan was kept secret. It was not in the papers. The belief that Jews are the enemy—yes. That Jews should be banished and so forth—yes.

"But Auschwitz and so forth and so forth were not that well known. Enough Germans knew. The Wehrmacht people knew. But not every German knew."

And what of Germany today? What are we to make of a nation and a society that cultivated the industry of genocide but one in which most of the perpetrators are gone?

"Germany today is surely not Germany of the past," said Wiesel. "On the other hand, you cannot think of Germany as a normal state, as a regular state, part of European and Western Europe. You cannot disassociate it from its past.

"On the other hand, I do not believe that there is something called collective guilt or collective innocence. There is no such thing. Which means the children of Germany are not responsible for what their grandparents have done to our people. They are not. Therefore, we should not treat them like that.

"I must have told you, sometimes in my classes I have German students and, very strange, because those who are feeling guilty shouldn't. And those who are innocent also shouldn't feel guilty. They shouldn't.

"But it will pass. In a few years, it will pass."

Indeed, in the next several years, as the last of the survivors and the last of the perpetrators leave us, we will be left only with the memory of what happened and the words and film footage and ephemera that document it. Inevitably the world changes, perspectives alter, but still the memory of it all lingers.

How can we ever think of Germany apart from the Holocaust?

Wiesel said that with the passage of time, we must recalibrate. "To say that the attitude of a Jew such as myself on Germany isn't changing constantly is wrong. It does change over time, because you expect something else, something different, from Germans today. I think there's a certain sensitivity which I expect to find both among Jews and among the Germans."

That's a far stretch from forgiveness. But perhaps it's as close as we can get.

16

How Shall We Regard Israel?

A cousin of mine who was a Holocaust survivor used to rush to see every Holocaust-related film the week it came out. He didn't miss one, and he told everyone about it.

I envied his emotional fortitude. Here was a man who had suffered starvation, witnessed death, and lost his family yet was willing to relive the experience in a darkened room before a screen that illuminated characters who were larger than life. I, on the other hand, had grown up in the comfort of mid-twentieth-century America and could hardly bear to see the movie trailers for such films, let alone sit through two hours or more of this agony.

Finally I had to ask my cousin, who long had been a personal hero of mine, "Why do you put yourself through this? How can you watch these films? I wince at the very thought of seeing them."

He did not hesitate in responding.

"I see them because I won," he said. "I lived."

Yes, indeed, the Nazis always lose the war at the end of these films, but Jews lost more. To watch these images through the prism of my parents' suffering is distressing. Thus I have never seen *Schindler's List* or *Shoah*, *A Beautiful Life* or *The Boy in the Striped Pajamas* and probably never will. I made it through *The Pianist*, but only because I watched it on assignment: the journalistic task at hand enabled me to go into work mode and put a bit of distance between the subject matter and myself. Still, the darkness of the film hovered for weeks. As it should.

Wiesel, like my late cousin, also watched these movies, but for a very different reason: Israel.

"I want to see them also—every movie," Wiesel said when I told him of my cousin. "And I read every book, simply to understand. Not because I won. I don't have that feeling.

"The only way we can think that we won is to think about the State of Israel. Go to Israel, you see what's happening there—one of the mightiest military outfits in the world. OK, it's a historical victory. But to say this is a victory over Hitler, this argument doesn't console me."

To Wiesel, Israel inspired a sense of triumph—not over Nazis but over the vicissitudes of history, a victory in the larger Jewish narrative and a culmination of Jewish nationhood. Yet this brings us to the tricky position of Israel in history, in the Holocaust, and in the world today—and how we children of survivors relate to all of this.

To this day, Israel often is described as compensation to Jews in the aftermath of the Holocaust. But that's a perilous way of looking at it. Yes, Israel emerged on May 14, 1948, and became a sanctuary to survivors rejected widely but accepted in limited numbers in America, Australia, Sweden, and other places. Yet to say that Israel was the world's way of providing reparation implies that these tragedies could be redressed, an unacceptable notion.

As Wiesel said during his lecture in Wisconsin in 1966, "Some politicians will tell you that there is a logic in events, that the State of Israel came into existence because of the Holocaust. Do not believe them. Maybe it is true chronologically, but it is not true, it should not be true, it cannot be true. Both events would be diminished by a comparison of this kind."

The linkage is indeed unsavory, even though it's often accepted as conventional wisdom. But of course, there can be no equating massive genocide with the return of a sliver of ancestral lands. Had Israel existed before the Holocaust, perhaps we could view the nation's relation to events differently; perhaps the connection would be more palpably real.

"It's true what some Israel leaders say: if there had been an Israel in 1939, there would have been no Holocaust," Wiesel told me. "They would have opened the doors, and that's it. Because the world closed their doors, Israel would have opened the doors. For me, therefore, Israel means something. But it's not a victory. This is not enough. The victory is not enough."

Nothing is enough, of course, to counterbalance what happened. The human calculus does not allow it. Moreover, the fact is that Israel, like the Messiah, did not appear on time. The chronology was off, with disastrous results.

"Israel came too late," said Wiesel. "And it wasn't Israel's fault. They could have come earlier," Wiesel added, referring to Jews who might have migrated to Palestine before the onslaught. Some, of course, did.

"They did, it was easy, so much easier [before the Holocaust]. But in the mystical language, we weren't ready for redemption. Just weren't ready, and therefore it came too late. The redemption came, but it was too late. I think Kafka said, 'When the Messiah will come, it will not be the last day, but the day after.' So Israel came a day after."

As Wiesel spoke these words, I remembered my father telling me that his family indeed emigrated from Poland to Palestine before the war, only to return to Europe, homesick. Had they stayed in Palestine, they could have lived. Because they returned, most were killed.

Wiesel, too, harbored regrets about such decisions made at the time, when no one could have imagined what others intended for them.

"Look, we had all the occasions to go there," said Wiesel, referring to Palestine. "We could have gone. Why didn't we? Who knows?"

We know: because it didn't seem necessary to the innocent.

"It wasn't," said Wiesel. "I didn't think it was. There was one family in Sighet, and they managed to go to Palestine from the ghetto. The ghetto was short-lived, but they were there in Palestine. It was possible to go there. To get a certificate is a matter of money. Why didn't we? Because nobody imagined the opposite. Nobody imagined really what it meant, the opposite of Israel, which was Auschwitz."

No one could have imagined that, except, of course, the inventors of the Holocaust.

But if we do not consider Israel a kind of payback after the Holocaust, how shall we regard it? What is Israel to us, the children of survivors? Is it a home for those who somehow survived and managed to build anew? Is it a symbol of Jews' determination to live, in the face of millennia of anti-Semitism? Is it a form of security, assuring the diaspora that there will always be at least one safe port before the next genocide? Regarding the latter, Israel indeed is becoming a sanctuary once again, this time for increasing numbers of French Jews in flight from rising anti-Semitism.

Wiesel was uniquely positioned to answer these questions, for he was in Israel in 1949 and returned uncounted times since. Moreover, Israelis held a deep connection to him, more than once urging him to become the country's president. It happened in May 2014, when Israeli prime minister Benjamin Netanyahu tried to rally support among ministers for a Wiesel candidacy before dropping the idea. And it happened in 2007, when officials approached Wiesel directly.

"It began with Prime Minister Ehud Olmert," Wiesel recalled of that time. "And he said, 'I have everything written. No campaign. Just say yes, and you will be the president of Israel.'

"I said, 'I am not an Israeli; I never lived there.' And the more I said no, you know how it is, the more pressure. So at one point, I went to Israel for Yad Vashem, and there was a press conference. I have never had such a coverage—my God it was political pressure.

"One journalist said something which hit me here," added Wiesel, tapping his heart. "He said, 'Professor Wiesel, aren't we good enough for you, so that you reject the highest honor that we can give you, to become our president?'"

A pained expression crossed Wiesel's face as he quoted these words.

"It was tough," he said. "Again, call it inspiration, call it God, spirit—but I found the right way to answer.

"I said, 'Ladies and gentlemen, why do you people come to me? For one reason alone: I have nothing except words. But they are mine. The moment I become president, they no longer are.'

"And that helped me. Otherwise I would be president. Let alone, my wife would divorce me."

So Wiesel stood deeply embedded in the meaning of Israel, a place that holds profound allure to many of us, though its importance didn't become apparent to me until the Six-Day War, when it seemed on the brink of extinction.

I asked Wiesel, What exactly is Israel?

"First of all, it surely means an event with miraculous dimensions, since it is here," said Wiesel. "Look—how to say it without betraying its very meaning? We could have lived our life without Israel. Now it's there. And because it's there, we cannot live without it.

"Does that mean that we should all pack up and go there? Of course not. But it surely means that the feeling is that we must do whatever we can to help Israel exist and survive, as much as we can, with every means possible. To even imagine now an event without Israel is impossible."

To Wiesel, Israel is indispensable to Jewish identity. To me, the place seems more important the more it is threatened, whether by perpetual wars with adversaries nearby or from enemies in Europe and beyond. For as long as I can remember, Israel has been the object of derision and attack around the world, receiving a measure of empathy only when it is under siege and on the verge of being vanquished.

"Israel has had some good times in the press. When Israel was threatened in 1967, the public opinion was on their side," said Wiesel.

Indeed, Israel's global popularity rises when it is in peril. During the Six-Day War, the Yom Kippur War of 1973, and the Persian Gulf War in 1991, when Iraq's Scud missiles were landing in Tel Aviv, sympathy for Israel around the world ran high. The world seems to love the country best when it's backed against a wall. When it successfully defends itself, less so.

The enduring woes and arguments over Israel will not be settled in these pages or any others any time soon, but let's at least explore the perspective of one survivor and one son of survivors.

I wince when I see how fashionable Israel bashing has become on university campuses around the world, including in America. During the war in Gaza in the summer of 2014, a Virginia Tech professor who had been on track to be hired at the University of Illinois in the American Indian studies program prolifically tweeted his thoughts on Israel and Jews.

Some of the commentary by Steven Salaita, as reported in the *Chicago Tribune*, was merely offensive: "If Netanyahu appeared on TV with a necklace made from the teeth of Palestinian children, would anybody be surprised?" "Let's cut to the chase: If you are defending Israel right now you're an awful human being." "Zionist uplift in America: every little Jewish boy and girl can grow up to be the leader of a murderous colonial regime."

But the professor had much more to say via Twitter: "Zionists: transforming 'anti-Semitism' from something horrible into something honorable since 1948." "You may be too refined to say it, but I'm not: I wish all the [expletive] West Bank settlers would go missing."

Not too far from genocidal phraseology, is it?

The University of Illinois derailed Salaita's appointment, and I was gratified that my newspaper, the *Chicago Tribune*, unflinchingly supported that decision. Pointing to the comment about West Bank settlers going missing, the *Tribune* editorial noted: "If that one doesn't strike you as reprehensible, substitute 'African-American' or 'gay' or 'women' for 'West Bank settlers' and imagine sitting in a classroom run by the author of that remark. Salaita also re-Tweeted a post from an account named Free Palestine, complaining that a story by journalist Jeffrey Goldberg 'should have ended at the pointy end of a shiv.'"

Salaita offered zero apologies for this eruption of hate and in fact published a defensive op-ed response in the *Tribune*. He asserted that "my academic career was destroyed over gross mischaracterizations of a few 140-character posts." Salaita didn't destroy his own career, in other words—everyone else did!

When I told Wiesel about this, he shook his head in disbelief.

In January 2015, Salaita filed a lawsuit in federal court against eight of the university's board members and several administrators and donors, claiming breach of contract and violation of his rights of free speech, according to the *Chicago Tribune*.

I bring this up to point out not only the venomous anti-Semitism that an accomplished professor felt no shame at promoting. Perhaps more disheartening was the wide support Salaita instantly received from many students, professors, and others. Campus chapters of Students for Justice in Palestine and the Gay Liberation Network organized a speaking tour of several prominent Chicago universities for Salaita. A petition demanding Salaita's reinstatement on Change.org drew thousands of signatures. Another, from the US Campaign for the Academic and Cultural Boycott of Israel (USACBI), saw more than twelve hundred scholars sign a petition vowing to boycott the University of Illinois on Salaita's behalf.

As often is the case, enmity toward Israel carries a certain chic on campus, notwithstanding the bigotry of the commentary being championed.

Salaita reached a settlement with the university in November 2015; the school paid him $600,000, plus $275,000 to his attorneys, and admitted no wrongdoing, according to the *Tribune*. Not a bad payday for Salaita and hate.

The affair crystallized the way Israel often is treated on American campuses.

"It's wrong," says Wiesel. "Israel is not the worst state in the world. Israel of course has made its mistakes, but which country hasn't? But to say that Israel is an evil country. It is not."

Yet Israel often is demonized by critics who are silent on human rights abuses from Hamas, Hezbollah, Gaza, Egypt, Syria, China, Russia, Cuba, and more. This hypocrisy is at the core of the Boycott, Divest and Sanctions (BDS) movement, in which some academic organizations target Israel—the sole democracy in the Middle East—while offering no such campaigns against dictatorships around the world. Vladimir Putin's Russia and Xi Jinping's China and Miguel Diaz-Canel's Cuba? No problem. Only Israel raises the ire of the boycotters.

Few have illuminated the bad faith of the BDS movement more brightly than Alan Dershowitz.

"There is nothing good about the BDS movement," wrote Dershowitz in the *Boston Globe* on December 27, 2013. "It is hypocritical, for singling out the nation state of the Jewish people for BDS, while ignoring other occupations (such as those by Turkey, China and Russia), as well as far worse violations of human rights and academic freedom, such as those committed by Cuba, Saudi Arabia, the Palestinian Authority, Russia, China and nearly all the countries of Africa. . . . It may also be illegal, since it discriminates on the basis of religion (it applies only to Jewish academics and business people in Israel, and not to Muslims), national origin and ethnicity. Moreover, BDS constitutes collective punishment, since it targets Jewish Israelis who oppose Israel's settlement policies as well as those who favor them."

Northwestern University law professor Steven Lubet echoed the point in an op-ed column in the *Chicago Tribune* on January 29, 2015, arguing that the Palestinian BDS National Committee supports a broad boycott "that would squelch academic freedom and institute nationality-based discrimination against Israeli scholars and schools. In fact, the published BDS guidelines actually oppose all events 'that are designed explicitly to bring together Palestinians/Arabs and Israelis so they can present their respective narratives or perspectives' and work toward reconciliation. Just Israeli/Palestinian programs would be permissible only if they promote 'co-resistance' rather than co-existence."

Yet the BDS movement persists. It amounts to a frontal attack on Israel and Jews under the guise of championing civil rights routinely crushed in dictatorships around the globe without comparable boycotts.

"I'm totally opposed to that," said Wiesel. "To single out Israel— really. It's not 'Israel and.' It's Israel. Oh, really? To single out Israel, as if Israel was really the worst democracy in the world, the worst regime, human rights violator—come on. This is so unfair, so unjust, so revolting. And I don't like it, and I don't appreciate it. I try to understand why. The reasons are not very flattering."

They are so obvious that Wiesel did not feel compelled to utter the word, but we know what it is: anti-Semitism. That's not to say that Israel is above criticism any more than the United States or any other nation. Is it not possible, though, to disagree with Israel's policy on, say, settlements without nursing hate, à la Professor Salaita, or selective/collective punishment, à la the BDS movement? Why the unique targeting of one remarkably successful country invented by one particular people?

"It was the fashion," said Wiesel. "But, look, I understand. I understand some young people who question Israel for all kinds of things. Why not? Israel is a democracy. What about the Palestinians? What about the Arabs and so forth? They are all good questions, and Israel is trying to answer. But to deny Israel's right to live as a state, a free state—that is beyond any acceptable argument."

Yet there remains the subtext of the BDS movement, the primary explanation for its singling out of Israel in a world thick with totalitarian regimes.

But it's not only the anti-Semitism of the BDS movement or hatred à la Professor Salaita that attempts to paint Israel in the most unflattering light possible. Often it's the peculiar dynamics of the media, a world I've been a part of my entire career.

During the Gaza War of 2014, American network television told a simplistic story day after day and night after night: bombs falling on Gaza, mere air raids in Israel. Pictures of carnage in Gaza, shots of glittering high-rises in Tel Aviv. Death tolls high in Gaza, quite low in Israel.

It was as if a sporting match were underway, and the side with the highest casualties must be the innocent victim and, therefore, the winner of the public relations war; the side with the fewest casualties must be the villain and, therefore, the loser in the eyes of media coverage.

As for context, who cares? As for who started the war, who cares? Andrea Mitchell on MSNBC expressed indifference.

"I'm not saying who started it . . . but the people who are caught in the middle are the people of Gaza," she said on TV in July 2014, in the midst of the fighting. "That's the asymmetry here."

Not saying who started it? Why not? Are those who started the war not responsible for putting the residents of Gaza in the line of fire? Apparently that doesn't matter. We live in a popular culture that presents conflict in simplistic terms unrelated to context, often reflexively casting Israel as perpetrator and Palestinians as victims.

Commentator Bill Kristol did not allow Mitchell's "who started it" dismissal to go unanswered.

"But we know who started it," he said. "This is not a mystery. It was started by Hamas. Israel has no interest, believe me, in going back into Gaza."

Nor did *Time* magazine's Joe Klein withhold fire on Mitchell's show. "I think that it's pretty well known that I've been very critical of Israel in the past," Klein said. But this time there has been "a failure of reporting on our side about the extent of the Israeli operation." He added, "This has been pretty well targeted."

Nevertheless, the American TV narrative consistently portrayed Israel as callous aggressor; NBC's chief foreign correspondent, Richard Engel, flatly called Israel's action "punishment" and Palestinians its victims.

"In truth, in certain ways they are," Wiesel said to me. "But not victims so much of Israel—but of their own leaders. They want to forget that in 1947 there was a partition grant, which Israel immediately accepted and the Palestinians rebelled," continued Wiesel, citing a history that emerged in no TV news reports I saw through constant viewing.

Let's recall an inarguable chronology: On November 29, 1947, as Wiesel indicated, the United Nations decided by vote to divide Palestine into separate Jewish and Arab states. Jews accepted this; Arabs rejected it. Egypt, Syria, Iraq, Jordan, Lebanon, and Saudi Arabia indeed launched a war to destroy their new neighbor.

"In 1948, Israel, before declaring independence, said, 'We stretch out our hand to the Palestinians, come and join us,'" said Wiesel. "If they had accepted, there would be a Palestinian state now, nearby. Lida would not be in Israel, would be in Palestine. Jaffa would not be in Israel. The smallest part of Tel Aviv would be Palestinian, and the Jews accepted it and wanted it and preached for it.

"The Palestinians didn't want it. They wanted a land without Israel."

And perhaps they still do?

"Some of them do, not all," said Wiesel. "Some, I'm sure, have learned, have learned the lesson."

That lesson being that wishing Israel out of existence will not make it so.

Except perhaps from the inside, if we believe some projections on demographics. But even here there is dispute. With 8.8 million people living in Israel, including 1.8 million Arabs, plus 4.7 million Palestinians in the West Bank and Gaza, demographic trajectories are not encouraging.

"Given current trends, there will come a day when the Arabs in Israel and the territories outnumber the Jews," wrote *Washington Post* columnist Eugene Robinson in July 2014. The trends Robinson referred to concern population growth, which is greater among Palestinians than among Jews.

No one can predict the future with certainty, but even the prospect of a minority Jewish state ruling over a majority Arab population seems morally and strategically unacceptable. So I asked Wiesel about Israel surviving as both a Jewish state and a democracy.

"What's wrong with that?" he quipped.

Nothing, of course, but is it really possible over time? Isn't the ticking clock working against Israel?

"Look, what happens one hundred years from now, I don't know," said Wiesel, getting more serious but sounding surprisingly sanguine—or hopeful—about the future.

"But for the moment, I can tell you, I go to Israel at least once or twice a year, if not three times a year, and I know what's happening in Israel. With all of the mistakes and all the faults, Israel is a democracy, first of all. A person who lives in Israel is a free person. A person can do anything that person wants, can go around in the street with banners attacking the government. No one will arrest him or her. So therefore, Israel is still the only democracy in that region."

Yes, I know. It seems obvious that an Arab in Israel has more freedom of expression and civil rights than in Egypt, Jordan, Syria, and elsewhere in the Arab world. Until he retired in 2017, Salim Joubran was an Israeli Arab serving on the Supreme Court of Israel for fifteen years. Not many Jews hold that position in the Arab world.

"Go prove, really," said Wiesel, meaning: try to tell this to the world. "There may be more yet to come. I trust Israel."

And yet the demographic numbers suggest there may be trouble ahead. Isn't Wiesel disturbed by these trends? I asked again.

"Let's talk thirty years from now," said Wiesel, perhaps preferring not to pursue this line of thought. "Come back thirty years from now. Come back," he said with a chuckle.

Ultimately, though, he was taking a broader perspective than I was. To me, each news report of a terrorist attack or of murmurings of another intifada evokes dread. Wiesel took the long view, seeing Israel's situation not in terms of days, months, or years but millennia.

"Look, one thing is clear," he said to me. "The Jewish people showed that it can survive tragedy, but it surely can survive democracy. Nothing is as alien to the Jewish people as dictatorship. Nothing. Because we suffered from dictatorship more than from anything else. Be it in ancient times, from the Babylonians and the Romans, and, of course, in our own time, in the twentieth century. We believe in democracy."

For this reason, many of us were distressed when former president Jimmy Carter published a book with the self-consciously provocative title *Palestine: Peace Not Apartheid*. Invoking the word *apartheid* in his title amounted to an indictment of Israel, or something very close to it.

Wiesel felt the same way and would not sit still for it.

"When he published his book called *Apartheid*, he called me up," remembered Wiesel. "And he came to see me: 'I'll come to see you privately. Why do I need Secret Service?'

"I arranged for him to come on a Sunday, when nobody is there in my office building. And I wanted my wife to be there. And he came with an assistant, so at least we had two and two," recalled Wiesel, in what sounded like preparations for an intellectual duel, each party bringing seconds.

"And for the first half hour, niceties, my importance to him and so forth. Very nice.

"And then I let him have it about the book: 'Mr. President. You call it apartheid in Israel. You don't even mention apartheid in your book.

Why the title? And second: I have been to South Africa before you. At that time, there was apartheid. That's why I went. I know what it is. You want the readers to make that comparison? I can criticize Israel for certain things. But apartheid?'

"And then I said, 'Mr. President, you actually in your book give the history of Israel. You don't mention the terrorist attacks. Not one?'

"I began giving example after example. And one father, a doctor—an Israeli doctor—he was specializing in emergency medicine, and he came back from a trip to New York to celebrate his daughter's wedding. So he took her out that evening, for the last time. His daughter was killed in a terrorist attack, and her groom came the next day to the funeral, and he took the wedding ring and put it into the grave. 'Did you write about it? Do you know how many other terrorist attacks there have been?'

"I gave him one after another. Phew."

The story of the ER doctor struck a familiar chord, for the murder of Dr. David Applebaum and his daughter Nava just before midnight on September 9, 2003, had resonated deeply in Chicago. Dr. Appelbaum, a father of two boys and four girls, had been ordained a rabbi at Brisk Rabbinical College in Chicago. He'd studied psychology at Roosevelt University in Chicago and received a master's degree in biology from Northwestern University, in the Chicago suburb of Evanston. He was part of us.

As *Chicago Tribune* reporter Colin McMahon's front-page story on Applebaum's death reported, the doctor worked "repairing bodies and soothing souls" at Shaare Zedek Medical Center in Jerusalem. He had just returned to the Jewish capital from New York, where he had taken part in a symposium to teach medical professionals how to respond to terrorist attacks.

Dr. Applebaum held precious experience in this field, for whenever these tragedies occurred, he would rush into action.

"He would appear at the site of every attack, volunteer, get in the ambulances to evacuate the injured to the emergency room," Dr. Kobi Assaf told the newspaper *Haaretz*. "I recall how he was distressed by the injured, by what he had seen, but again and again, at night, he would be there."

On the night of September 9, one day before his daughter Nava was to be married, Dr. Applebaum returned to Jerusalem and took her out for cake at the Hillel Café.

"The night before the daughter gets married, the father wants to have a little time with her," Aviva Kashuk, a family friend, told the *Tribune*.

As father and daughter sat together, a Palestinian believed to have been a member of Hamas forced his way in before midnight and set off a suicide bomb. As always, the doctors at Shaare Zedek Medical Center looked for Dr. Applebaum to appear at any moment.

"When David didn't show up immediately to treat the victims . . . my heart sank," Dr. Jonathan Halevy, the hospital's director, said in a eulogy. "And then when the family arrived and said that he and Nava had been at the café, my heart sank even more."

Chicago's Jewish community, and others around the world, mourned his death and his daughter's.

"There are thousands of people who owe their lives to him—thousands," Rabbi Louis Lazovsky of Congregation Kesser Maariv in Skokie told the *Tribune*. "To say that he was like an angel of God, an angel of mercy coming in, is not an exaggeration."

Whether such stories, told by Wiesel, had any effect on Carter only the former president knows. The two men spoke occasionally, Wiesel said. But clearly, Carter is not alone in diminishing Israel's side of the perpetual battle it has fought for its existence since its emergence seventy years ago.

As Wiesel said in the aforementioned United Nations speech, "Those who today preach and practice the cult of death, those who use suicide terrorism, the scourge of this new century, must be tried and condemned for crimes against humanity. Suffering confers no privileges; it is what one does with suffering that matters."

Nevertheless, Israel as always finds itself surrounded by adversaries who do not necessarily wish for this democracy to endure. That is why Wiesel appeared in full-page ads in the *New York Times*, *Chicago*

Tribune, Washington Post, and other major newspapers urging the United States to prevent Iran from going nuclear, he said to me.

"I appeal to President Obama and Congress to demand, as a condition of continued talks, the total dismantling of Iran's nuclear infrastructure and the regime's public and complete repudiation of all genocidal intent against Israel," Wiesel said in the ad. "And I appeal to the leaders of the United States Senate to go forward with their vote to strengthen sanctions against Iran until these conditions have been met."

Wiesel said he heard from supporters around the world after the ad began appearing.

"I got such a response to that," he told me. "And what do I say? Come on: Iran cannot become nuclear. It's very simple. You cannot trust Iran with nuclear weapons. They have enough weapons. What else do you need? Why do they need nuclear weapons, really?"

Unfortunately I believe we know why. It has everything to do with a tiny nation called Israel and which people created that nation. And yet, when it comes to the Middle East, once again Wiesel saw possibilities where others observed despair.

"I am optimistic," he said to me, a remarkable observation in light of all he had said on the subject. "You know, I organized a lot of conferences—Nobel conferences. And once in Jordan, King Abdullah [II] of Jordan, we did four Petra conferences. And at the first one, in 2005, I invited Prime Minister Ehud Olmert and Palestinian president Mahmoud Abbas to come together. And when they met for the first time in our presence, they fell into each other's arms, and they sobbed like children. I had chills.

"I turned to my wife and said, 'Now I believe that peace is possible.'"

That peace still has not come. The Iran nuclear deal that Wiesel argued against was completed, and the United States subsequently withdrew from it.

And no one had more reason to give up on the future than Wiesel and his generation of survivors, who suffered so much for the identity that Israel embodies.

Yet Wiesel maintained hope, a lesson for the rest of us.

17

Further Thoughts on *Night* and Its Implications

It turns out that the gentleman who sat facing me for four years, addressing questions central to both of our identities, had struggled with the same paradoxes, wrestled with the same contradictions, and often arrived at the same quandaries that we children of survivors confront. Wiesel couldn't necessarily reconcile Jewish morality with humanity's self-inflicted tragedies any more than we can, but he certainly held up the problems for examination through the light of his experience and study.

To the reading public, his book *Night* stands as an evocative portrait of shtetl life before the Holocaust and a devastating account of his profound journey through it, one man's unflinching view of what happened, articulated in words that Wiesel himself found lacking but that many of the rest of us consider shatteringly real. Irving Abrahamson, an author who collected many of Wiesel's writings in the three-volume set *Against Silence: The Voice and Vision of Elie Wiesel*, put it to me this way: "He takes you up to the doors of the Holocaust—and then he takes you inside." "*Night*," added Abrahamson, is "a short book that contains a whole world that existed once and that was destroyed."

It also conveys the terrors of those times, or at least as much of it as words can hold, as readers can bear, and as Wiesel himself could capture. There doesn't seem much left to say after its 120 pages have ended, and yet we continue to need to say more, to learn more, and, above all, to ask more. Surely the world came to know Wiesel through *Night*, even if it took two generations before the book's truths became evident to millions.

Perhaps it's worth noting that *Night*, unlike any of Wiesel's other volumes, originally was written in Yiddish, a language of heightened pungency, ferocity, and poetry. As Wiesel said to me, "That was my language, my first language—I was born in Yiddish. It's my homeland. You can describe Jewish suffering in Yiddish better than in any other language. Suffering or humor. It's either laughing or tears, in Yiddish."

Mostly the latter in *Night*. But a very different language was spoken in Auschwitz, said Wiesel.

"It was another language created there," he said. "The language of the land of death. A strange language. I could speak to Greek, to Jews, Italian Jews, totally alien from my little place, Sighet."

To me, in part it's the stark, stripped-down, sinewy language of *Night*, as well as its tightly coiled narrative, that moves us. Plus, of course, the fact that its unnerving observations only can hint at what Wiesel and my father and mother and so many others experienced during those years. Wiesel, as I've mentioned earlier, didn't tell us everything, and what remained unspoken proves as chilling as what was expressed. Or more so. What Wiesel left out in this most telegraphic of memoirs plays darkly in our imaginations.

In a way, Wiesel's strategy mirrors what our parents did, leaving out so much, refraining from telling us stories that were too painful for them to recount and too onerous for us to hear. Even at this late date, after so many millions of words in so many languages have been expended on the Holocaust, most of the story remains untold, beyond the realm of language and comprehension. I believe this is what Wiesel was trying to tell us when he said he did not speak of certain things that happened to him and to the others, just as our parents also stayed silent about so much, for so long.

The effects of these events obviously are lasting, and that's apparent not only in the way my parents behaved in our little Skokie home. To me, one of the most telling passages in *Night* unfolds during the death march to Buchenwald that Wiesel described, a harrowing trek from one nightmare to another that I imagine was similar to my father's perilous trek to Buchenwald at the same time.

En route, Wiesel and the emaciated men plodding through snow and ice arrived in Gleiwitz, too many bodies suddenly crammed into too small a space, "a dark barrack where the dead were piled on top of the living."

And from this place where lives were crushed by extinguished lives, where victims were stacked atop victims, a teenaged Wiesel gasped for air and strangely heard a few strains of Beethoven's Violin Concerto. They were played by Juliek, a young man Wiesel had met in Auschwitz and who also found himself on the verge of being suffocated. Yet Juliek somehow had kept his fiddle with him and scratched out a few of Beethoven's notes.

Wiesel knew the music well. He, too, had played the violin as a boy in Sighet, starting at age nine, and he, too, had played Beethoven's Violin Concerto, he told me. Even here, in the midst of this carnage, one young man a few notes from death cried out with music. Since reading this passage, I cannot hear the Beethoven Violin Concerto without thinking of this moment. By morning, Juliek was dead, both his instrument and his body crushed.

"When I saw his violin there," Wiesel told me, "I said, 'I will never touch the violin again.'"

He did not. One more sign that for the survivors, the Holocaust never really ended.

I told Wiesel that by chronicling such an event, by speaking out for humanity—just as Juliek did with his violin in the last moments of his life—Wiesel has become to us children of survivors and to many others a kind of moral authority in the world.

Wiesel wholly rejected this idea and that position.

"I am nobody's conscience," he said to me. "Everybody has his own conscience. With all my weaknesses and my faults and my transgressions, come on, I'm not a saint. Don't make a saint of me. I am not all that. I am not a symbol. A symbol is not human."

Instead, Wiesel said he saw himself as a witness, a storyteller, a teacher. Even so, he conceded that he sometimes wondered what would have happened if he had taken another path. As we sat together one afternoon in Florida, the sun glinting off the blue-gray waters outside his hotel, he pondered aloud what he might have become if he had not chosen to write and speak and teach. Characteristically, though, he viewed his options through the lens of his faith and its narratives.

"Look, let's say if I had to choose a kind of profession, what would it be?" he asked himself, aloud. "Would it be a commander like Joshua? Would it be a prophet like Isaiah? If I had to choose a profession? Again, every one of my generation, which is your generation as well, at one point you must make that choice, to say, 'Hey, what would I do? What would I do, now, fifty years later? What else could I do with my life? What could I have done?'"

I suggested that perhaps he might have become a musician, perhaps a conductor. Following the war, Wiesel had led choirs, after all, a joyful experience for him, judging by his memoirs. In his early days after his liberation, Wiesel organized a vocal ensemble in France, building upon what he learned in his musical studies as a child and from singing in the synagogue in Sighet.

"My choir attracted quite a few people," he wrote in his memoir *All Rivers Run to the Sea*. "The most beautiful girls in the home joined, and suddenly I had more boys than I needed."

Like Wiesel, my father found solace in music after the war, playing the Hohner accordion he acquired while recuperating in Wiesbaden. I know that if my father had had the chance, he would have become a musician, because music was for him—as it is for me—a balm, a healer, a way of expressing what words cannot.

As for himself, Wiesel was skeptical.

"What good would it have done for humanity if I knew how to conduct an orchestra?" he asked me. "There are greater ones than I, and, therefore, actually destiny said no.

"My work, if it has any weight, it should be words. After all, I live with words, so certainly my choice would be linked to the world of words, with certain prerogatives.

"Meaning I always believe that the worst sin I can commit is the sin of humiliation. Which is to be rejected, no matter what. There is no reason in the world that could justify my decision to use words to humiliate other people. That I know. I know it's not what I want. I think this is what I try to teach my students and my readers."

To Wiesel, in other words, his life's calling was not simply to use words but to use them in a particular way. Earlier, I referenced Wiesel's statement that "words can sometimes, in moments of grace, attain the quality of deeds." But he also remained committed to the reverse: words that avoid a particular deed—humiliation.

Considering that humiliation was integral to the Holocaust—Jews were not only slaughtered but also demeaned and dehumanized on their way to their deaths—perhaps that's not so surprising. But Wiesel regarded humiliation as far more important than society typically does today. To him, it was central to the way we should think about humanity.

"It is a great issue," Wiesel said to me, perhaps noticing my surprise at the importance he placed on this word and what he said it signifies. "Ultimately it is *the* most important issue of this generation, or our generations in plural. No doubt in my mind. No doubt because of the implications. There are so many possibilities and situations that could be applied to this one."

The dictionary defines *humiliate* as trying "to hurt the pride or dignity . . . by causing to be or seem foolish or contemptible." This pales alongside Wiesel's description.

"Humiliation is, of course, an injury, but it goes beyond that," he told me. "Because it humiliates the very being. Therefore, it has the word *shame* in it. We have no right to do it, to bring shame to another.

"Whatever we may say to express our difference of opinion, of feeling, anything, one thing I have no right to do is to humiliate someone. Because it's so easy and so tempting, to show one's superiority to the other."

I hesitate to think of the humiliations my father and mother suffered during the war, these injuries to their sense of self delivered not quickly but chronically over the course of many years—at least from 1939 to 1945 (though they faced humiliating anti-Semitism long before that). Then, too, in the years after the war, when they struggled haltingly to learn a new language in order to survive, when they worked menial jobs to earn enough to eat. Wiesel also often told me of the many days of hunger he experienced walking the streets of Paris after the war.

It does not surprise me that he wished to avoid afflicting others with such shame, for he, like many survivors, had felt its sting twofold: for himself and for those around him. More specifically, for his father.

"In camp, he suffered, knowing I had witnessed his humiliation," Wiesel said to me. It pained Wiesel, in other words, not only that father and son were humiliated but that the father saw the son watching the father's humiliation.

Thus Wiesel considered this issue an overriding concern, especially for children of survivors who suffered such indignities. A certain deduction can be made here: if you remove humiliation, you remove the sharp edge of bigotry, and you disarm its ultimate end point, genocide.

For Wiesel, this notion was not a mere academic exercise. After the war, the choice to humiliate—or not—was real, for his beliefs along these lines were put to the test. While covering the Eichmann trial in Israel in 1961, Wiesel happened to recognize a *blockalteste*—the head of a concentration camp barracks where Wiesel and others subsisted. It's not difficult to imagine the rage that would have risen up inside anyone in such a moment. Now Wiesel could strike back. He was free. He could lash out. He could say what he thought, without fearing for his life.

"At that point, I had a choice to humiliate him or not, in the bus," said Wiesel.

He considered the possibility. And he made the choice that I now knew he would make—to avoid shaming this man.

To accost him verbally was something "I wouldn't have done, which I didn't," said Wiesel.

Humiliation, Wiesel felt, was not his right. Even so, Wiesel characteristically will not tell the rest of us how we should act.

"Is that now a philosophical choice, which I would suggest to be accepted by others, in other situations as well?" Wiesel asked. "Who am I to do that? You can say, of course, any judge can issue a judgment. Any prosecutor is doing that, actually, saying, 'This guy should be humiliated. Not only punished—humiliated.'

"Why should I do that? But it opens a door to a lot of questions: Could we today, seventy years later, say, 'OK, now the time has come to open the door to humiliation'? Why not? I meet in the bus somebody who was a *kapo* [a prisoner who supervised other camp prisoners]. Is it proper, is it right" to confront and humiliate them?

To Wiesel, clearly not. The humiliations that he and millions of others suffered during the Holocaust did not give license to return such behavior, he insisted. To the contrary, the humiliations he received showed him that we must go another way.

I wish I could say that my extended family of survivors had come to the same conclusion. But most of them treated one another with such contempt that I eventually realized their behavior was a visceral reaction to their Holocaust experiences. Having been abused so badly during the Holocaust, they tormented one another verbally and emotionally ever after. I say this not in judgment but in regret, their actions another legacy of what they endured.

Wiesel appeared to have taken a very different path, which may explain the many times he spoke to me of something he valued highly in human endeavor. "I believe in friendship," he said. "To me, friendship, it's a cult. It's a religion."

Friendship, added Wiesel, "is underrated. Everyone thinks love, love, love, the religion of love, the life of love. Friendship is as important if not more important—but different. Pure friendship.

"Friendship is—I wrote somewhere, and Marion is so angry when she hears it," said Wiesel, referring to his wife of more than forty-five years, with a touch of tongue-in-cheek. "I wrote, 'Friendship is more important than love.' In a strange way."

But isn't friendship love?

"It's a kind of love," said Wiesel. "Nevertheless, friendship is almost beyond love. It's about—love is something immediate, and there's something physical about it. Not with friendship. Friendship is evolved. It's more curious."

As always, Wiesel developed this thought in his writings. As a narrator in *The Forgotten* says, "After all, wasn't friendship stronger than love?"

I asked Wiesel if he held friendship in such high esteem—seemingly in a realm unto itself—because of his Holocaust experience. Surely friendships forged under such dire circumstances resemble no other relationships and perhaps create a template for friendships yet to come. Might his fervent view of friendship have been shaped by the tragedies and miracles he experienced and witnessed?

"Everything is enhanced by my experience," said Wiesel. "Whatever I do now, whatever I say now, whatever I think about now, it cannot *not* be influenced by that. But I imagine that before [the Holocaust], friendship was important to me. My first friendships mean something."

At this point, I had to show Wiesel something I knew I would bring to him sooner or later. I reached into my briefcase, pulled out a slender white envelope, and delicately plucked out an old black-and-white snapshot I'd found in my father's old photo album. It was a small, head-and-shoulders picture of a very thin young man. Written on the back was an indecipherable name and these words: "Buchenwald, 1945."

Ever since I found this photo, after my father's death, I have wondered about this man. Obviously he was a friend of my father's from Buchenwald, likely a friend he never saw again. Certainly this was no one my father ever mentioned to me. But my father valued this friend enough to cling to this photo—and none other of anyone from Buchenwald—and carry it with him from the ruins of Poland to his recuperation in Germany to his new life in America. From the past to the present to the future.

Wiesel's face melted at this photo.

"Yah, yah," he said. "This is August 1945. I must have known him," Wiesel said of the man in the photo, "because he was young," as was Wiesel. The man pictured and Wiesel and my father were at the same place, at the same terrible time, and now they were linked anew by the yellowed picture in Wiesel's hand and by my inquiry about it.

Who was this friend of my father's from Buchenwald? And why is it that the more I learn about what happened, the more I realize I don't know, the more stories seem to slip through my grasp?

"You will find one day," said Wiesel, holding out hope. "You will find one day. Some stories are still unfinished."

To Wiesel, the ghosts of the past—like the one captured in the photo of my father's friend—pervade the present.

"I remember something very strange," he said to me, referencing the day in 1986 when he received the Nobel Peace Prize.

"During the ceremony, the world is watching. And all of a sudden I had a feeling I was seeing my father. I couldn't speak," he said with a sigh. "Long, long endless minutes passed. His eyes never leave me, and my little sister's, they don't leave me. And all that fused into the Nobel. What am I doing here? So many of my peers, of my family, are not there, and I am there? What am I doing there?"

"The mystical world" always hovers, as far as Wiesel was concerned, and to underscore the point he told me the story of a friendship he forged in Buchenwald. Menashe Klein survived and went on to become an important and prolific rabbi. The two men spoke regularly on the phone for decades. No matter where in the world Wiesel was, he would call his friend in Brooklyn, where Klein lived most of his postwar life.

"He was a very important rabbinic authority, and he became a very pious rabbi," said Wiesel. "And I told him my problems. And surely you cannot say I am a religiously pious person. But nevertheless, our relationship never suffered. And one day, eve of Rosh Hashanah, I get up usually very early in the morning, say my prayers, and in my prayer there are a few names—the prayer for the sick, for the ill. And he was one of them. And I forgot him—the prayer for his recovery.

"And then, eleven o'clock: 'Oh, God! I forgot his name in my prayer.' I ran to the telephone, called. Answering machine: 'The funeral left.'"

The mystical connection between friends had not been broken, Wiesel contended, least of all by death, a thought he would explore further.

18

The Magical Power of Memory

While turning the pages of the Sunday *Tribune* one afternoon, I noticed a letter from a reader that surprised me. The author was contributing to a standing feature called A Love Story in 100 Words, and she touched on a mystery regarding memories of an event that preceded her existence, and mine.

She had been on vacation when a man she did not know approached her and asked, "Are your parents European?" she wrote. "I looked at him incredulously and answered, 'Yeah. Why? Are yours?'"

That the gentleman should have discerned in her face "European" features was not so remarkable, nor that his parents also were from that continent. But it was something more specific and potent that drew him to her.

"After talking for hours comparing notes about our Polish Holocaust survivor parents," she wrote, "I went back to my room at 4 a.m., woke my roommate and told her, 'I'm going to marry that guy.'"

A year later, they were indeed married, and twenty-six years later remained so, the parents of "four beautiful sons and wonderful memories."

But a very particular memory—that of their parents' suffering and survival—pulled these two together. If, as Wiesel has said, words can attain the quality of deeds in moments of grace, then in this moment a memory of events that occurred before either of these two was born became a palpable force in drawing them to each other.

Because Wiesel had done so much to reclaim the memory of those who were destroyed and to cherish the power of memory, I had to ask him how he interpreted this story of the two children of survivors who found each other through their hitherto unspoken but shared pasts. How did this happen?

"One memory appealed to another," said Wiesel. "The dialogue of memories. Memory has its own mystery and its own mysterious power. Memory proves clever enough to share itself in other memories, whether you know it or not. Maybe it is being done in darkness, but it's being done. It goes from generation to generation."

The darkness Wiesel referenced surely represents our lack of awareness of the memories we carry with us, memories of catastrophic events we never witnessed but that nevertheless are deeply embedded in our identities as children of survivors. It took me practically until I was fifty, after all, until I began to recognize the memories that my mother was running from on the night she fled her house. Once I opened that gateway into her story, long-forgotten memories of my childhood with her and my father rushed in.

When I stepped onto the grounds of my mother's dying city of Dubno, when I proceeded into the home where she had spent a few innocent years, when I walked through what remained of the Jewish ghetto where she had suffered as a child before fleeing for her life, I was touching the memories that eventually had undone her. Those memories, of course, always had been hovering in the background of her life, and mine, though I was quite late to recognize it.

We are repositories of the past, and the letter to the *Tribune* describing two children of survivors who found each other represents but one instance of the animating force of memory.

Wiesel offered another. "I'll give an example," he said to me. "I was fascinated for a long time with the Spanish Inquisition and its consequences.

"From time to time, we discover a family that for the last three hundred, four hundred years were Christians. All of a sudden, they really become Jewish. Why? Because they remember that Friday evening for them is a very special evening," even though they don't know or remember why.

"Later they began searching and realize they come from a Jewish family."

Having learned that Friday night is sacred in the Jewish tradition, Wiesel explained, they begin searching for their roots, eventually embracing a Judaism that has been latent in their family for centuries. A fragment of a memory regarding the importance of Friday evening leads them to their family's pre-Inquisition identity.

This theme of memory as a power unto itself—something that travels in the dark through generations and epochs—echoed in Wiesel's writings, often intertwined with the meaning of Judaism. Wiesel expounded on this motif of post-Inquisition revelation in his story "Testament of a Jew from Saragossa," from his book *Legends of Our Time.* In this narrative, developed from a real-life incident, Wiesel went to Spain for the first time, intrigued by "those enigmatic priests who, in the name of love and for the sacred glory of a young Jew from Galilee, had tortured and subjected to slow death those who preferred the Father to the Son."

Wiesel was inexorably drawn to this place, where a foreshadowing of the Holocaust had occurred, and he was fascinated by particular victims of the Inquisition: Marranos—Jews who were forced to convert to Christianity, though many continued to practice their Judaism in secret. He admired the duality of their lives, he wrote in "Testament," because "by deciding to stand their ground on two levels simultaneously, they lived on the razor's edge, in the abnegation of each instant."

Wiesel's first trip to Spain led him—by coincidence or fate—to a poor Catholic man who approached him on the street and offered to be a tour guide. After the two began conversing, Wiesel wrote, the man realized Wiesel was a Jew and insisted that Wiesel come to the man's home. There the fellow produced a piece of parchment roughly four hundred years old. It had been handed down through the man's family, one generation after another, but the man could not decipher the language.

Might Wiesel be able to help? The precious document, it turned out, was in Hebrew and had been penned during the Inquisition.

Wiesel translated it aloud, word for word, including this sentence: "I, Moses, son of Abraham, forced to break all ties with my people and my faith, leave these lines to the children of my children and to theirs, in order that on the day when Israel will be able to walk again, its head high under the sun, without fear and without remorse, they will know where their roots lie."

The document—passed through the family's generations as if it were an amulet, "the disappearance of which would call down a curse," wrote Wiesel—established that the Catholic man was in fact a Jew by heritage. This shocked and appalled the man at first, but soon he hungered to know more of his family's nearly buried past.

So Wiesel told him the long and winding story of the Jews: the Inquisition, the roots of Judaism, the First Temple, the Second Temple, the battles of Jerusalem and Masada, Auschwitz, modern-day Israel. Ancient memories—hidden but preserved in plain sight in a sheet of yellowed parchment—were reawakened, the man eventually renaming himself Moshe ben Abraham: Moses, son of Abraham.

Neither time nor circumstance had eradicated memory. It lives in us. But why?

"I don't know why, but it happens," said Wiesel. "Which means our memory is not lost. It would be a sin, as much as a mistake, to witness its disappearance. Memory is not lost. And therefore we cling to it, and we try to enrich it, as well as we can, always. And therefore it's individual, personal, but also collective."

The concept of memory permeates Jewish existence, Wiesel maintained. How did Jews communicate through the generations before Gutenberg invented the printing press? Through memory: each Talmudic school had a memorialist—someone with an exceptional memory who could retain everything that was said. The Old Testament phrase "In the beginning," Wiesel said, links Jews to the memory of prehistory.

"If there is a leitmotif" in Jewish life, Wiesel added, it is memory. Without it, "there is no culture. Without memory, there is no metaphysical endeavor."

But thanks to memories that live through epochs, the man in Saragossa with the telltale parchment rediscovered his family's ancient past, and the two children of survivors in the *Tribune* letter found one another.

"Without memory, nothing exists," Wiesel said to me. "I'm sure it can be said about other religions as well, but we Jews especially, we are defined by our memory, and by our link to memory, by our passion for memory. The word that is the most frequent in our culture, even biblical culture, is *remember*. As a Jew, we know that we live thanks to memory. *Zachor*: Remember. Remember. Remember."

The theme resonates in Wiesel's writings, as in a scene from *The Forgotten*, in which the protagonist—an American journalist—tries to explain to his German translator why he is fasting on Tisha B'Av, which marks the destruction of the Temple in Jerusalem.

"You can't be serious," says his translator. "Your temple was destroyed two thousand years ago and you're grieving *today*?"

"Yes," says the journalist, "as if it happened only yesterday."

She responds that the Jews must be crazy, and even though the Jewish journalist whimsically concurs, she continues to protest.

"It's human nature to forget what hurts you, isn't it? Wasn't forgetfulness a gift of the gods to the ancient world? Without it, life would be intolerable, wouldn't it?"

"Yes," says the journalist, "but the Jews live by other rules. For a Jew, nothing is more important than memory. He is bound to his origins by memory. It is memory that connects him to Abraham, Moses, and Rabbi Akiba."

When the character Elhanan gets married in *The Forgotten*, in the midst of the fight for Israel's independence, in Jewish custom he "smashed the glass under his heel in memory of the Temple's destruction." Memory permeates our rituals and our existence.

Perhaps this is ultimately why we sons and daughters of survivors return to the places where our parents' families were destroyed: to try to reclaim memories they have not been able to share with us. To "breathe the air you breathed," a survivor's son says in *The Forgotten* to the spirit of his father, who has sent him on a journey to an ancestral village. To "see the sights that made you drunk," to "take in fragments of memory that have been chipped away from yours."

We preserve memories in other ways, too. As in the very names that we children of survivors bear, most of us named for those who did not live. I am named for my father's father, whom we believe was killed in Auschwitz. My sister, Barbara, is named for my mother's mother, who like most of the rest of my mother's family lies in the pits of Dubno. Their lives echo in our names.

"A dying man takes his soul with him but leaves his name to the survivors," says Gavriel, the protagonist in Wiesel's novel *The Gates of the Forest.*

"The Germans don't know to what extent they are branded by their stupidity: they kill off Jews but they can't find a way of erasing their names. The Talmud teaches us that deliverance will come because Israel has not changed its name. It is not by chance that God is known as the Everlasting; every name has something immortal and eternal about it which defies time. Day follows night and night follows day, men are born and die, but the most fragile things—for what is frailer than a name?—endures."

Through these names, "they live," Wiesel said to me, referring to those who were killed for being Jews. "And that's why I wear my grandfather's name. What remains of the people?" he asked. "Naturally the history—the history is in the names."

But eventually, through the generations, I said to Wiesel, I fear that the names inevitably dissolve into the vast sweep of history, or at least their meanings do. The second generation will give way to the third and fourth and fifth, the memories that the names represent eventually vanishing into a generalized accounting of events summed up in textbooks. The names may live, I told Wiesel, but the individuals they represented will be forgotten, wiped away.

He disagreed. "Howard, first of all, we Jews have a strange way of remembering," he responded. "All our holidays are based on memory.

Passover, on the Seder they are supposed to say, 'Our ancestors were slaves in Egypt.'

"My ancestors! Do I remember my ancestors?" Wiesel added with a laugh. "Slaves. I say, 'We were in Egypt.'"

Nonetheless, Wiesel added, "We remember with such precision the destruction of the Temple in Jerusalem, and we observe the ninth of Av, Tisha B'Av. They are fasting to this day for an event that happened more than thirty-five hundred years ago. I can give you the details, the names of the generals. We remember with all the precision. We are going to forget what happened seventy years ago? I am not worried."

As always, Wiesel held out hope where I saw very little.

"Howard, again, you and I belong to a strange people," he said. "And our people [are] filled with tears and with joy and with sadness. The memories that are made of these tears are actually part of your own."

There are some memories, however, that even Wiesel acknowledged might lie beyond his optimism and humanity's reach. These are the events that happened in towns unlike my mother's Dubno, where at least a few dozen of the twelve thousand killed survived to tell the story. In other places, no one did. No one can tell us what happened and to whom it happened. No stories or diaries or pieces of parchment unlock the past. No Yizkor book documents for all time the sorrows of these execution grounds.

"The real sadness, the tragic sadness is what about those cities or villages that didn't leave any witnesses, because they killed every last one," said Wiesel, perhaps running up against the outer edges of his otherwise inextinguishable hope.

And yet he hastened to cite memories that somehow survived despite staggering odds: the stories of the *Sonderkommandos*—Jews forced to toil in the gas chambers at Auschwitz, watching their victims proceed to their fiery deaths and handling the remains after. Most of these *Sonderkommandos* eventually met the same fate as the others, but a few survived. And remembered, and gave witness.

"I think that the most frightening testimonies were written by the *Sonderkommander*," said Wiesel. "The *Sonderkommander* were those who did the burning—not killing—but the burning. And I remember seeing them [in Auschwitz]. Although they lived alone, the Germans kept them and fed them. After three months, usually the *Kommandos* were killed. Except the last ones. In Birkenau and in Treblinka, there were people from the *Sonderkommando* who kept diaries.

"One of them was in Birkenau. If you read that—for weeks I couldn't sleep," continued Wiesel. "One of them wrote that he had just seen his own community, and among them were members of his family. And the question was, Should he tell them that they were already on the way to gas chambers?

"One of them was a Dayan, a rabbinic judge, his name was Leib Langfus," said Wiesel, speaking of a man whose notes were found after his death in Auschwitz.

"You cannot imagine what this man saw, in the shades of the flames, which consumed our people and his family. The other fellows of the *Kommandos* allowed him to daven and to study and so forth, and to write his memoirs. There? There?"

Even there, in the most heinous place humanity has known, memories were preserved. If memories from such a place can survive, Wiesel seemed to be saying, then the memories of what happened surely will live as long as humanity endures.

The memories will survive literally, in the form of writings from survivors such as himself, and in less tangible forms, passing ineffably from one generation to the next, from the Inquisition to the Holocaust, from parent to child to grandchild, a force that we cannot understand but that plays on our imagination nonetheless.

As Wiesel says, we remember.

In that, I believe he found cause for hope.

Afterword

I always hoped and presumed that Wiesel and I would be together when the book of our conversations was released. Perhaps he even might have written a foreword, raising the curtain on what we had done together and on the four most illuminating years of my life.

When the manuscript was finished, he asked me to send it to him in Florida, then come visit him again, so we could discuss it. With some trepidation, I packaged it up and overnighted it to his hotel, wondering if I had done justice to our rich and expansive dialogue.

A few weeks later, I arrived in Florida, checked into my hotel, and called him to find out when I should come over.

"I'm eager to talk to you about the book," I told him over the phone.

"It's good. It's very good," he said, offering me much-needed and immediate relief.

Still, I looked forward to poring over the text with him. Would he wish to reconsider any of his quotes? Would he want to say anything in a different way? Would he object to how I had interpreted his thoughts or expressed my own?

When we met in the hotel lobby, we embraced, as always, but I was surprised by what I saw—or didn't see: he wasn't holding the fat black binder I had sent him. Perhaps he had forgotten it in his room.

"Do you want to go over the manuscript?" I asked him once we sat down in our usual spot.

"No," he said pleasantly.

"Really?" I asked.

"No, it's very good. Nothing to change."

At this moment, I felt immensely pleased and slightly disappointed, because I had been savoring the opportunity of poring over these pages with him, analyzing word choices and discussing sentence structures and debating historical concepts with the most compelling thinker and writer I ever had known or ever would. Then, again, I was moved to realize that I had not let him down with the words I had put to paper.

That matter dispensed with, we continued as we always had, talking about the news of the day, the latest outrages against humanity, the music we both had been listening to and I had been writing about. He never ceased to marvel that, as a *Chicago Tribune* critic, I could attend any concert I wanted, obtaining the best seat in the house at a moment's notice, simply by placing a phone call or sending a message.

"I envy you," said the Nobel laureate whose literary works were admired around the world and who surely would be welcomed in any concert hall, almost anywhere on the planet, whenever he wished.

I continued to visit Wiesel in Florida and New York. Each time, he asked me to come back to spend more hours with him than I'd requested, to add another session or another day to our encounters. When we weren't in the same city, we talked on the phone, laughing, lamenting, never lacking for subjects to analyze or decry.

The last days we spent together, in Florida in the winter of 2016, felt like simply another profound experience in a long series of them, an ongoing conversation I wrongly assumed would continue uninterrupted for years to come. But as we walked downstairs from the lobby of his hotel toward the pool area in back, he complained of being winded and paused a couple of times to catch some air.

"Last year, I could go down these stairs like nothing," he said to me. "Now I am out of breath."

I gave too little attention to his complaint, perhaps not wishing to acknowledge that after all his travails, struggles, losses, achievements, and exertions around the world, this eighty-seven-year-old man finally was slowing down. Even Elie Wiesel, who had endured Buchenwald with my father and had attempted to answer questions I never had been able to ask my parents, might be approaching an end I did not wish to foresee.

So we proceeded to the terrace facing the crystalline waters of the Gulf of Mexico. Wiesel leaned back into a lounge chair, and I sat at the end of it, speaking what would be my last words with him face to face.

It was quite warm out, and he had rolled up the sleeves of his light blue shirt nearly to his elbow. I couldn't help noticing that a napkin was thrown over his forearm, covering the tattooed number he had acquired in Auschwitz. Was this by happenstance, I wondered, or intentional? I did not ask, but I guessed the latter.

We spoke of some of our favorite subjects, including the great pianist Arthur Rubinstein. Wiesel told of having received a phone call from Rubinstein when both were in Paris, the musician having seen Wiesel on TV. Rubinstein asked for a meeting, and if I recall correctly, they had lunch together. Immediately I wished I could have witnessed this meeting, two giants of the twentieth century in conversation, one having transformed how we think about Chopin, the piano, and "love of life," as Rubinstein always put it; the other having given the world tools with which to grapple with the genocide from which both he and Rubinstein and millions more had suffered.

I mentioned that Rubinstein, whose family in Lodz was murdered during the Holocaust, refused for the rest of his life to perform in Germany or to perform with musicians with Nazi ties, such as Herbert von Karajan. Silently we both nodded our admiration of a choice few others of Rubinstein's stature had made.

We spoke, too, of Johannes Brahms and Vladimir Horowitz, of Hillary Clinton and Benjamin Netanyahu, of cold weather (which he disliked) and chocolate ice cream (which he loved) and, inevitably, of the miracle of our meeting and friendship.

Then we bid each other farewell, promising to meet again in New York. After that, we conversed on the telephone.

I was in my home office writing one afternoon in 2016 when my phone buzzed, and I learned the awful and, to me, unexpected news that Wiesel died on July 2. It just wasn't possible. I instantly recalled an imperishable quote from writer John O'Hara: "George Gershwin died on July 11, 1937, but I don't have to believe it if I don't want to."

Neither do I. For Wiesel's words still echo in my ear every day, little different than if he still were here sitting next to me.

Acknowledgments

M y work with Professor Wiesel on this book was aided and encouraged by so many, including Mrs. Marion Wiesel; Marissa Poock and Adrienne Mansard in Professor Wiesel's office; *Chicago Tribune* editors Gerould Kern, Colin McMahon, Geoff Brown, Scott Powers, Jennifer Day, Lara Weber, Robin Daughtridge, and Elizabeth Taylor; *Chicago Tribune* photographers Nancy Stone and Zbigniew Bzdak; Chicago Review Press editors Yuval Taylor and Ellen Hornor; editor Lisa Reardon; copyeditor Julia Loy; Jennifer Joel, my longtime literary agent; Bill Young of Midwest Media; Willard G. Fraumann and the Chicago Humanities Festival; and Pam Becker, my wife.

Index